TEDIOUS JOURNEYS

Studies in the
Postmodern Theory of Education

Joe L. Kincheloe and Shirley R. Steinberg
General Editors
Vol. 375

PETER LANG
New York • Washington, D.C./Baltimore • Bern
Frankfurt • Berlin • Brussels • Vienna • Oxford

TEDIOUS JOURNEYS

Autoethnography by Women of Color in Academe

EDITED BY Cynthia Cole Robinson
AND Pauline Clardy

PETER LANG
New York • Washington, D.C./Baltimore • Bern
Frankfurt • Berlin • Brussels • Vienna • Oxford

Library of Congress Cataloging-in-Publication Data

Tedious journeys: autoethnography by women of color in academe /
edited by Cynthia Cole Robinson, Pauline Clardy.
p. cm. — (Counterpoints: studies in the postmodern theory of education; vol. 375)
Includes bibliographical references.
1. African American women college teachers—Social conditions.
2. Mexican American women college teachers—Social conditions.
3. Educational anthropology—United States. 4. Racism in education—
United States. 5. Discrimination in education—United States.
I. Robinson, Cynthia Cole. II. Clardy, Pauline.
LC2781.5.T43   378.1'2082—dc22   2009037347
ISBN 978-1-4331-0768-9 (hardcover)
ISBN 978-1-4331-0767-2 (paperback)
ISSN 1058-1634

Bibliographic information published by **Die Deutsche Nationalbibliothek**.
Die Deutsche Nationalbibliothek lists this publication in the "Deutsche
Nationalbibliografie"; detailed bibliographic data is available
on the Internet at http://dnb.d-nb.de/.

The paper in this book meets the guidelines for permanence and durability
of the Committee on Production Guidelines for Book Longevity
of the Council of Library Resources.

For all the women of color
in higher education
who travel along this academic journey
with the tenacity to endure

TABLE OF CONTENTS

Chapter Five

Chapter Six

Chapter Seven

Chapter Eight

FOREWORD

Annette Henry

I voraciously read *Tedious Journeys*, savoring every word, recalling my own personal memories of institutional injustice as a professor, memories that lay hidden as a personal strategy to continue the important work that I believe we need to do in academe. I also recalled many of the stories of Black women that I had researched for more than 20 years, and how they negotiate their spiritual and academic lives, teach against the grain, and work for structural and educational change. The day–to-day practice that many women of color carry out in classrooms and in administration is at its most powerful when told in first-person accounts such as these in *Tedious Journeys*. At the same time, I pondered how much work has yet to be accomplished in terms of equity and justice. Indeed, students and colleagues will point out that Barack Obama is the U.S. president, or that Oprah Winfrey is one of the most wealthy and successful businesswomen in the world, or even that their vice-chancellor is a Latina; surely, racism and sexism are not terribly relevant in contemporary American society! Lest we think that we have arrived as a nation, these authors remind us that the journeys and the struggles continue. Reading about the everyday lived experiences of Latina, Mestiza and African American women in academe reminds us that although there is much "talk" about diversity, the difficult work of confronting racism/sexism and inter-group racial/ethnic conflicts are rarely broached. The journey is so tedious that many Black and Latina colleagues in colleges of education frequently play with the idea of returning to teaching in the public school system.

These are powerful first-person accounts of the meanings of Black, Latina and Mestiza activism in the classroom and in administration.

These authors share the painful personal and political consequences of their pedagogies, profession choices, and philosophical
positions. I am thrilled that these women of color are presenting
their stories in engaging auto-biographical and auto-ethnographic
ways—ways that will resonate with scholars across fields and
generations.

Do not be fooled by the title. While *Tedious Journeys* explores the
experience of Black and Latina professors in higher education, these
accounts resound with the hope of change. Although their journeys
may at times be emotionally, spiritually, physically, financially and
familially taxing and toxic, these scholars do not give up, or give in.
They continue to find creative ways to work in spite of structural barriers, to find support from sisters, family, friends, God, and the
strength that dwells within every woman whose materiality is sur-
rounded by White supremacist, patriarchal, classist thinking. We
have a dichotomous existence in universities, at once striving to make
a difference and change the consciousness of our students and colleagues, indeed the very nature of academe, all the while struggling
against the institutional readings of our Black and Brown bodies in
the workplace and the superficiality of many diversity initiatives.
Alas, the more things change, the more they remain the same. We are
still used and set up so that those in power can feel good about their
"new minority hires." How shocked they are when women of color
decide to leave, or dare to question, or "talk back" to racist and sexist
allegations by students, staff and faculty or write autoethnographies
about race and gender inequities!

The authors warn that we must practice self-care, that the kinds of
issues for which we advocate, and the kinds of oppressive situations
we find ourselves in, can take a toll—even life-threatening—on our
health. Being tenured or a full professor does not make one's journey
any easier.

Audre Lorde (1984) reminded us that we were never meant to survive. Yet these women find ways not only to survive but to live fully, and embrace the importance of their work and the unique perspectives that they bring.

Annette Henry
University of Washington, Tacoma
July 12, 2009

PREFACE

Cynthia Cole Robinson and Pauline Clardy

"Pauline, you know I feel like I'm experiencing Post-Traumatic Stress Syndrome though I'm not there anymore (former university). I know I need to move on, but it just seems so hard," I said as I unplugged my cell phone from the car charger and activated my Bluetooth earpiece to continue my conversation. "I think that I need to write about it, not in a scholarly way, but start journaling or something as a way to come to terms with it."

"I know what you mean, I feel the same way," she sighed. "I think about it sometimes and I regret how much time I spent there. They had me so weighed down with administrative stuff that I never had a chance to write. Now I have to try to make up that time in publishing. At least you got a semester in which you didn't teach to work on your book."

"Yeah, that was one good thing that I have to give them—they gave me time to work on writing that term. If it wasn't for that time, I wouldn't have gotten anything done. But that's when Colleen was running the department and she believed in being an advocate for the faculty. She was a rebel. I have to realize though, as long as she had been there, she had the clout to make some things happen. With new administration comes change, and they need to prove points and impress the right people," I sarcastically added.

"In my department, I felt as though they were just piling it on. Sometimes I felt like they were just looking for a warm body to run those programs that they came up with willy nilly," Pauline continued.

"I know what you mean," I huffed as I was taking my morning walk and talking about three octaves higher as I always do when I get excited or angry about something.

"Like the time they put me on the university planning team so that I could speak about issues of diversity and didn't listen to a thing I had to say. I was driving two hours just to speak but not be heard. It's like I wasn't even in the room. I would say something and it would be like, 'Umh, that's an interesting point.' Ten minutes later a White faculty member would say almost the same thing and it was like the best thing since sliced bread. Then the draft of the minutes would come out the next meeting and my comments wouldn't even be there. After I saw what was up, I just stopped talking. As soon as I could get off that committee I was out of there. They wanted my name on the membership list to show that they had representation from faculty members of color, but they really treated me like I was invisible. I figured I could save my time, wear and tear on my car and protect my blood pressure," I added. "I would be so frustrated that I would have to pop a Motrin just to make the drive home."

"Yeah, I felt the same way in the meetings that I attended. I know I didn't say much but the minutes never mentioned anything that I said. And remember those meetings we both used to go to our first year at the school district and neither one of us knew why we were there?" Pauline almost can't get it out before she starts to laugh. We both burst into laughter. It was hilarious to reflect over the years with the experience of knowing eyes.

"It's good that we can laugh about some of it. Maybe we'll laugh about the rest of this crap someday, but it's hard to imagine." I added, though I don't know if I even believe that day will come.

"Laughing is better than crying," she said.

"But for real though, I think I really need to write about it, you know, unedited and see what I come up with."

"Are you thinking about writing it for publication or something?" Pauline asked.

"I don't know. It's hard to tell the whole truth about the things I've experienced," I answered. "I'm thinking about backlash."

"Well, you're not there anymore, what can they do?" she asked.

"Yeah, I guess that's true. They do know that they have issues with retaining faculty of color. That academic climate study that they gave to the faculty last year showed that they had major issues with job satisfaction and belongingness among minority faculty. I know I tore them up on that survey. I almost wanted to fill it out twice!" I laughed.

"I didn't know about the survey. That must have taken place after I left. Maybe they want to do something about retaining faculty of color. They are losing good people," Pauline said.

"Anyway, the ratings were so low that the president even mentioned it at the faculty all-call. You know that's something 'cause they usually try to keep stuff like that on the low. They even put together a focus group of faculty of color to get more information about it. But I don't know what was up with that because they only invited certain people. They probably didn't invite me because they knew what I was gonna say after how they played me with that unequal pay for the same work crap." I said getting charged up once again.

"Yeah, the pay is a serious issue. You know it was really hard for me to make ends meet when I was working there. I had a Ph.D. and I felt like a pauper," she said. "I was making more money when I was a classroom teacher and a graduate student."

"I know what you mean. And just to think, they were paying White men without Ph.D.s more than they were paying me. If it hadn't been for that email that Tom sent out about average salaries at similar institutions and average pay within our institution, I wouldn't have ever known. That's the thing about private schools—they don't have to disclose that stuff." I added.

"Yeah, and all that stuff they put you through when you brought it to them," Pauline reminded me.

"Talkin' about, 'you have to negotiate that up front.' That's such crap. That's just a matter of equity. They know full well that they were paying me less than people who didn't even have Ph.D.s. That was discriminatory and they know it. I remember telling Colleen about it and she asked me if I thought it was racial or gender discrimination. I told her, 'hell, what does it matter? The Equal Employment Opportunity Commission (EEOC) ain't gonna bother to split that hair,' as if one was more acceptable than the other."

"Really," Pauline added in agreement.

"Anyway, that's probably why they didn't invite me in on the focus group. They knew what I was gonna say. Plus they probably still wondering if I'm gonna file a suit. Remember when Stan took over the department. He asked me if I had any issues and I told him about the unequal pay thing. He asked how much I made and he agreed that I was being underpaid. Even though he piled all that administrative crap on me without considering how it was making it impossible to do research, he did have my back on that. He really stuck his neck out there to try to get it righted."

"He did, and that couldn't have been easy being new to the position and all," Pauline added.

"Yeah, I know. After a high-ranking administrator refused to correct the pay difference, Stan got real nervous. Remember when he asked me if I was gonna file a suit? He was like, 'I know you're gonna get the best legal minds money can buy.' I just didn't respond, he was like, 'don't sue me.' I know he went back and told them I was probably going to sue. The truth is I would rather leave than go through all that mess. But after thinking about it, it became less about the money and more about the social justice issue. It's like I couldn't stand being there after that. My morale was so low; it was so hard just to go to work. I felt like I was in pre-civil rights America. Something like that really hits you in the gut. It was just too hard to get over. I gave them all I had and they really had won me over with the collegiality talk, but the stuff they pulled sure wasn't collegial. That was straight up discrimination—I think it was race, age and gender." Do you think I should write about it?"

"Girl, yeah. You're making me remember now. It's been a year for me so I kinda just put it out of my mind, but it would be good for you to begin to work through it. But if you want to actually do something with it like make a paper out of it, I'd be interested in working on it as a project because what we have to say as African American female professors will speak volumes about our needs as faculty. And if diversity is truly a goal of these institutions, our voices need to be heard."

This "life note" or "over heard conversation" as Dillard (2006) terms it was the genesis of this project and our journey towards the willingness to be vulnerable by sharing our life stories or autoethnographies about our experiences in the academy as African American women academics as a more authentic way of exploring diversity in the academy.

Introducing the Autoethnographies

This book is divided into two sections. Section one consists of an autoethnographic study conducted by Cynthia Cole Robinson and Pauline Clardy. Their research examines the experiences of two female African American professors in the culture of predominantly White institutions. It also explores racism and sexism embedded in the cultures of the universities and how they affect the professors' experiences within the institution as well as in the classroom as teachers of a majority White student population. The purpose of the research is to lend voice to the experience of female professors of color as a means of creating a dialogue and developing support networks for women of color who may have similar experiences and increase institutions' awareness of how female faculty of color actually experience life within the academy. The availability of experiences of faculty members of color can aid in institutional efforts to move beyond the rhetoric of diversity to the practice of diversity; hence, increasing the attraction and retention of faculty members of color. Each chapter in this section opens with an excerpt from a spiritual, which is reminiscent of W.E.B. Du Bois' *Souls of Black Folk* written over a century ago. This is intentional as spirituality has historically been and continues to be a source that many African Americans tap into to navigate the marginalizing culture of society and its institutions.

Chapter one contains a brief history of diversity in higher education, a literature review on the Black female professoriate, Black Feminist Thought as the theoretical framework, autoethnography as the methodology and data analysis. Chapters two and three are thematically-based autoethnographies of Cynthia Cole Robinson and Pauline Clardy, respectively, which describe their experiences as assistant professors in a predominantly White university in the Midwest.

Section two contains chapters contributed by other female professors and administrators of color. It begins with chapter four, "Migrations through Academia: Reflections of a Tenured Latina Professor," by Maura Toro-Morn. This chapter contains a brief account of the institutional history of Illinois State University and its efforts at attracting minority faculty. In keeping with the title of the chapter, the author describes how migration and border crossing have shaped her teaching and scholarly work and how this border crossing experience has shaped her development as a scholar and her vision of the future of the academy. Additionally, the chapter contains a narrative that focuses on the author's experiences in two classroom settings.

Chapter five, "'Are We Change Agents or Pawns?' Reflecting on the Experiences of Three African American Junior Faculty," by Michelle Jay, Catherine L. Parker-Williams, and Tambra O. Jackson uses autoethnography as a medium to understand, analyze, and make meaning of the experiences of three African American female junior faculty members working in a predominantly White institution. Drawing on data that include in-depth phenomenological interviews, reflection journals, formal/informal dialogues, and official documentation, the authors explore a notable predicament that occurred during their second year in the academy and its subsequent impact on their professional and personal identities as well as their day-to-day existence within the college. The dilemma, which is detailed in a narrative format, highlights the conflicts that inevitably result from the daily negotiation between their self-imposed identities as scholar/activists and thus, "change agents," and the "agents of change" identity imposed upon them by their colleagues and administration.

Chapter six, "What Does Racism Look Like? An Autoethnographical Examination of the Culture of Racism in Higher Education," by Adah Randolph is an autoethnographical study that seeks to examine her experiences of racism in the academy, by exploring how these experiences of racism become "normal" and how a culture of racism has manifested and been supported institutionally in the academy through human interactions, in meetings and in the classroom setting. Finally, she ponders if the culture of racism has changed in the academy. Her research is grounded in history, higher education, critical race theory, the concept of cultural capital, and Black feminist theory.

Chapter seven, "'We Are Not the Same Minority': The Narratives of Two Sisters Navigating Identity and Discourse at Public and Private White Institutions," by Ayanna F. Brown and Lisa William-

White, is an experimental narrative employing Critical Race Feminism and autoethnography to illustrate the complexities and at times, conflict between the authors' identity and *minority* status, and the *minority* issues touted as essential to social justice initiatives within and beyond their respective campus departments. Enacted in this chapter are the stories of two sisters, both of whom pursued careers as teacher educators at predominantly White institutions within departments that articulate a commitment toward social justice. The authors illustrate how their familial bond and shared academic interests allow them to navigate these circumstances and create support systems within and beyond the dynamics of their departments, universities, and the academy.

Chapter eight, "Women and Minorities Encouraged to Apply Challenges and Opportunities of Critical Cultural Feminist Leadership in Academe," by Alicia Fedelina Chávez explores the leadership experiences of a Mestiza in higher education. Teaching stories are used in the tradition of Spanish and Native American cultures to illustrate some of the ways of being, challenges, and opportunities of a woman of color negotiating predominantly White and predominantly Spanish and Native American collegiate institutions and communities in the Southwest and Midwest.

The women whose stories appear in this volume answered an open call to female scholars of color in academia. The autoethnographies which are included are written by African American, Latina and Mestiza (Spanish and Native American) women. Their stories are in their own voices, and they do not profess to speak for all women of color, nor all women who share their races/ethnicities.

Reference

Dillard, C. (2006). On spiritual strivings: Transforming an African American woman's academic life. New York: SUNY.

ACKNOWLEDGMENTS

I am a patchwork quilt of so many hands that helped to weave me into the woman I am today and for all their efforts, work and commitment I must give thanks. Though my mother only lived for the first seven years of my life, she left a presence of strength, courage and tenacity that guides and sustains me today. I am grateful to all of my aunts who offered examples of compassion, dignity and grace that only sepia tones of passing time can foster. To my othermothers and mentors, particularly Annette Henry, who have helped me through trying times and my academic journey I say thank you for their selflessness and wisdom. I offer gratitude to my cousin, Debra, who was a great support during my earlier years in the academy and all my sistah friends who are always there to help me make sense of a world that often leaves us with too many questions and prompts our endless search for answers. I acknowledge my brothers, James and Stephen, who are a constant reminder of how far we've come together and provide me the warm and loving comfort that can only come from the home one knows as an innocent and eager child. Thanks to my husband, Dion, for his unwavering support. Finally to my daughter Payton Olivia and my nieces Taylor, Morgan, Jordan and Kennede who are too young to understand this work now, I pray that they will find a smoother, well-paved road when their brown faces enter the halls of the ivory tower. It is my desire that this road to and through the academy will not be tedious when it is time for their journeys but soft and malleable beneath their feet.

Cynthia Cole Robinson

Giving honor unto God who is the head of my life, I am thankful for the angels that He strategically placed in my paths to help me along my journey. I acknowledge Drs. Karen Sakash and Victoria Chou for making my graduate studies possible and helping to mold me into the teacher that I am today. I offer my gratitude to all of the phenomenal women of color who have contributed to my success in higher education. Their stories of strength and endurance have inspired and motivated me to stay the course. Specifically, I thank Dr. Flora Rodriguez-Brown who opened many doors for me and served as my mentor as I was introduced to the academy. I also thank Drs. Irma Olmedo and Annette Henry for the many lessons that they taught me as women of color in academe. Next, I acknowledge Dr. Phyllis Metcalf-Turner, who in her position of Department Chair has been a role model for me.

I also acknowledge my colleagues in bilingual education, Drs. Elizabeth Skinner and Andrea Montgomery and Maria Luisa Zamudio for their support and friendship. To my wonderful students who are too numerous to name, I recognize you for the lessons that you have taught me along my journey.

I am thankful to my siblings, Joe, Linda and Angie and my cousin, Ruby for their prayers and unconditional love. To my aunts, Mexie and Mary, and my uncle, Daniel, I say thank you for being there for me whenever I have needed you. I acknowledge all of my nieces and nephews, particularly Pauline, Hope, Retha, and Giovanni, the children that God blessed me to share. To all of my friends, I say thank you for your unwavering support and encouragement. Finally, I acknowledge the most phenomenal woman of all—my mother, Mattie Murdock—for giving me life and preparing me to be the woman that I am today.

All of the aforementioned people and many more that I have encountered throughout my life's journey have helped me navigate the roads, hills and valleys that I have passed along the way. Thanks to these people I can repeat the words of Dr. Maya Angelou, who wrote "Wouldn't Take Nothing for My Journey Now."

Pauline Clardy

Section One

CHAPTER ONE

Introduction

Cynthia Cole Robinson and Pauline Clardy

Walk with me Lord; walk with me.
Walk with me Lord; walk with me.
While I'm on this tedious journey,
 I want Jesus to walk with me.

Be my guide Lord; be my guide.
Be my guide Lord; be my guide.
While I'm on this tedious journey,
Be my guide Lord, be my guide.

Don't leave me alone Lord; don't leave me alone.
Don't leave me alone Lord; don't leave me alone.
While I'm on this tedious journey,
Don't leave me alone Lord; don't leave me alone.

A Negro Spiritual

Diversity in academia is in its adolescence. When we peruse the history of diversity in the academy, we find that desegregation trickled into the educational system some fifty plus years ago and that diversity among university faculty enjoyed a drop here and there, but not until the seventies did African Americans begin to receive professorial appointments at predominantly White institutions at a rate of 4.7% in 1981 (*Journal of Blacks in Higher Education*, 2007) and African American women professors were even more scarce. While there are some collective experiences among African Americans in the university, African American female professors have unique experiences that stem from the intersection of race and gender, i.e., double oppression (hooks, 1989). The work of African American women professors is well articulated and set against the backdrop of Black feminism (Collins, 2000; Guy-Sheftall, 1995; hooks, 1989; Lorde, 1984; Omolade, 1994). Like the developmental phase of adolescence, this is a period of expressing voice, exploring the complexities of identity, full-out resistance to the status quo and "diversity for NCATE's sake." For those of us who are among the small number of women of color in the academy, we continue on our quest of making meaning of our experiences and our purposes within this place and find that much of that purpose and meaning is found in who we are as a people, as African-descended persons. This is often the passion and fuel that drives us in a place that is arid of acceptance of difference, yet moist with misunderstandings and misconceptions around issues of race and gender.

The research in section one examines the unique lived experiences of two female African American professors in the culture of predominantly White institutions. It also explores the presence of racism and sexism embedded in the cultures of the universities and how they affect the professors' experiences within the institution as well as in the classroom as teachers of a majority White student population. While universities seek compliance with diversity mandates and standards, many times they are ill-prepared on how to attract and retain faculty of color (Alex-Assensoh, 2003; Myers & Turner, 2001; Turner, 2000). Also, initiatives are undertaken by institutions to address issues of diversity, but all too often the initiatives are present in written policy but not reflected in the operations of the university and among the predominantly White faculty. As a result, faculty members of color experience racism and discrimination in the institutional structure as it relates to the hiring processes, committee appointments, promotion and tenure, collegial relations among colleagues, etc. In the classroom, African American female professors experience racism in the form of disrespect from students who resist multicultural curricula with social justice orientations, challenge the professors' authority and demand to authenticate their "right" or qualifications to teach (Ladson-Billings, 2005; Vargas, 2002). The purpose of this research is two-fold: (1) we hope to lend voice to experiences of female professors of color as a means of creating a dialogue and developing support networks for faculty members of color who may have similar experiences. Such experiences can be isolating and debilitating and support networks and validating stories often can assist professors, especially new faculty members, in negotiating the marginalizing university cultures we describe. (2) This research can increase institutions' awareness of how faculty members of color actually experience life within the academy, which can aid in institutional efforts to move beyond the rhetoric of diversity to the practice of diversity; hence, increasing the attraction and retention of faculty members of color.

Legacy of Research on the Black Female Professors

Literature that mentions the Black female professoriate tends to be folded into larger discussions about: 1) faculty of color in the academy; 2) diversity and the recruitment and retention of faculty of color; and 3) women in academia. Few studies are focused primarily on the unique experiences of Black female faculty in the academy. One reason for the paucity of literature in this area of research is the small percentage of this population who teach in majority White universities. Faculty of color, both male and female, tend to work at community colleges, historically Black colleges and universities as lecturers or non-tenure track faculty members (Alex-Assensoh, 2003). Vargas (2002) refers to statistics on race and ethnicity in the U.S. professoriate as "slippery" (p. 23), because there is no differentiation between foreign-born and native-born professors. According to Vargas, universities do not make this distinction because it helps them appear to comply with the regulations for representation of underrepresented minorities.

Beyond the Big House: African American Educators on Teacher Education, is an example of writing that focuses on the lived experiences of Black female professors. Gloria Ladson-Billings (2005) features seven prominent Black female scholars who discuss their experiences in White majority institutions. The author uses "The Big House," as a metaphor to connect their experiences to those of slaves belonging to a plantation/institution but lacking the power and privilege of those in the mainstream. Treated primarily as a part of a larger context, literature that pertains to Black female faculty will be discussed in the rest of this section.

The Journal of Black Studies published an entire issue on race in the academy in September 2003. In it, Yvette Alex-Assensoh (2003) discusses incorporation in the academy, a concept that is used in political science and urban politics, to take diversity to a level of power sharing and institutional change. Alex-Assensoh states that diversity is often seen as tokenism, and its effects are questionable if the result is not institutional change. She lists sub-processes for incorporation (p. 8): (a) full access to institutional resources (b) representation in college and university administration (c) active involvement in departmental and college-level policy making (d) implementation of ethnically and racially egalitarian policies (e) greater parity in terms of tenure, promotion and salary outcomes. In an article by Caroline Turner in the same issue of *The Journal of Black Studies* (2003), she discusses the lives of female faculty of color who have experienced some level of incorporation in the academy as being filled with "lived contradictions"—to be a professor is to be White; to be Black (or anything else) is not to be White—and "ambiguous power" as they experience constant challenges to their authority from students, parents, colleagues, etc. According to Turner, what gives these women of color some sense of satisfaction is their "love of teaching, sense of accomplishment, contribution to future scholarship, and opportunities to mentor and be mentored" (p. 116).

Regina Dixon-Reeves (2003) discusses mentoring as a precursor to incorporation and found that African American male professors tend to mentor African American graduate students and junior faculty more readily than African American female professors, stating that the latter's time is usually consumed with service and other family-related or household responsibilities that women have. She calls for male and female professors of color to renew their commitment to mentoring emerging scholars of color and to "continue to fight against attempts to marginalize their research and to devalue their service and activist contributions to the academy and their surrounding communities" (p. 23).

In an another article in the September 2003 issue of *The Journal of Black Studies* entitled, "Visible and Invisible Barriers to the Incorporation of Faculty of Color in Predominantly White Law Schools," Victor Essien (2003), discusses barriers that could also apply in other realms of academia such as colleges of education, i.e., being a part of a hostile environment that does not support faculty of color or their research, being burdened with committee work which is given little importance when tenure decisions are made, failure to mentor faculty of color, leaving faculty of color out of "the information loop," not being hired or promoted because of race or ethnicity and inaccessibility to resources. The greatest barrier that Essien cites is racism, which he places at the core of all manifestations of institutional barriers to incorporation in the academy.

In "Race, Research, and Tenure: Institutional Credibility and the Incorporation of African, Latino, and American Indian Faculty,"

James Fenelon (2003) discusses how some universities that depend on private endowments from alumni do not support the incorporation of faculty of color because their research tends to focus on race and is viewed as controversial. This lack of support is made manifest in promotion and tenure decisions and resources.

In the area of diversity, there are pressures on universities to recruit a more diverse student population, to prepare students to live and function (as teachers, lawyers, etc.) in a diverse society, and to recruit a diverse teaching faculty. According to Smith et al. (2004), the area in which universities tend to miss the mark in terms of diversity initiatives is the recruitment and retention of a diverse faculty. Much of the literature on the recruitment of faculty of color suggests that the lack of faculty of color is the result of few students of color earning doctorate degrees (Myers & Wilkins, 1995; Norrell & Gill, 1991, Ottinger, Sikula, & Washington, 1993; Schuster, 1992; Solórzano, 1993). This shows that efforts in the area of recruitment of students of color and the mentoring of these students to support them in furthering their education beyond the baccalaureate and masters levels are of great importance in leading to the diversification of faculty.

In a study of 700 searches, Smith et al. (2004) studied whether specific interventions led to the hiring of faculty of color. Smith and colleagues contend that hiring members of underrepresented groups happens under these conditions: (1) The job description used to recruit faculty members explicitly engages diversity at the department or subfield level; (2) An institutional "special hire" strategy, such as waiver of a search, target of opportunity hire or spousal hire, is used; (3) The search is conducted by an ethnically/racially diverse search committee. Their results confirmed the first two hypotheses; however, the third could not be analyzed due to a lack of diversity on search committees.

According to Tack and Patitu (1992), women professors experience more stressors on the job and in their personal lives than men.

As a result, they have less job satisfaction. These authors contend that in order to attract and maintain women in the professoriate, something has to be done to enhance job satisfaction, the rewards system, and ways in which universities help faculty deal with personal life situations. Otherwise, they could become "an endangered species." Tack and Patitu (1992) also claim that minority female faculty are less likely to be tenured, often hold low-ranking positions with low salaries, have a heavy service and advising load, are unsupported in their work, feel isolated, and experience discrimination.

An article by Thomas and Hollenshead (2001) entitled, "Resisting from the Margins: The Coping Strategies of Black Women and Other Women of Color Faculty Members at a Research University," includes the results of a survey on faculty members' work lives and career satisfaction based on these themes: (1) organizational barriers; (2) institutional climate; (3) lack of respect from one's colleagues; (4) unwritten rules that govern university life; and (5) mentoring (p. 168). The results indicated that more Black women and other women of color reported organizational barriers as hindrances to their careers; cited feelings of being used in an unfriendly, non-collegial and non-supportive atmosphere within the institution; identified a lack of respect for their research by their colleagues; reported not having access to information that they were later required to adhere to as a common unwritten rule; and cited lack of a mentor for career support as pervasive among women of color. Coping strategies that some of the respondents mentioned were being an advocate for self, which includes learning how to negotiate for salaries and speaking up for oneself. Another strategy was to network with other similarly situated African American female professors to give one another affirmation and support. An additional strategy was to refuse to allow someone who does not have respect for one's research agenda to dissuade or make one change her focus or research agenda. A final strategy was to protect oneself from service overload, especially if tenure has not been attained.

Black Feminist Thought

To address the phenomenon of interest in section one, the lived experiences of two female African American professors at predominantly White institutions, we utilized Black feminist thought (BFT). BFT emerges out of the exclusion of the concerns and voices of African American women from the mainstream feminism movement, which probably can be more accurately identified as the White feminist movement (Collins, 2000; Lorde, 1984). BFT spans across the cultures and disciplines into fields such as Sociology, History, Ethnic Studies, Education and Women's Studies (Cole & Guy-Sheftall, 2003; Jarret -Macauley, 1996; Oyewumi, 2003; Steady, 1999; Terborg-Penn & Rushing, 1996).

BFT applies to the field of education in the following ways: First, BFT acknowledges the centrality of gender and how it intersects with other forms of subordination such as racism and classism. This is relevant to our study because as African American women, we experience the "double oppression" of being African American in a society that has historically oppressed people of African descent and as women, we experience the patriarchal oppression that remains to be prevalent in our society (hooks, 1989). Secondly, BFT challenges the "mainstream" epistemologies and paradigms by proposing new ways of knowing and understanding the space we occupy as African American women professors in a largely White and male profession (Collins, 2000; Dillard, 2006). Third, BFT has a commitment to social justice and service as well as a research agenda that is intended to lead to the elimination of sexism, racism and other forms of oppression. Fourth, BFT acknowledges the importance and centrality of the experiential knowledge of women of color and views our stories as legitimate and pertinent to teaching about sexism, racism, and other forms of oppression.

BFT helps us analyze sexism and racism at macro and micro levels as they affect the society and impacts the academy. It also enables us to identify the individual and institutional forms of sexism and racism and its collective impact on the individual and the group. BFT provides an alternative to dominant epistemologies and allows us to make meaning of our experiences through our particular worldview. Therefore, we look to BFT to guide us as we analyze our lived experiences as African American female professors and sexism and racism in the academy.

Methodology

Autoethnography

Methodology should complement the theoretical lens used to frame the study. BFT was born out of the need to voice the unique experiences of African American women living in American culture (Collins, 2000; Guy-Sheftall, 2003); therefore, autoethnography is fitting as the methodology as it connects the personal lived experiences to the cultural. As Ellis and Bochner state, "back and forth autoethnographers gaze, first through an ethnographic wide-angle lens, focusing outward on social and cultural aspects of their personal experience; then they look inward, exposing a vulnerable self that is moved by and may move through, refract, and resist cultural interpretations...in these [autoethnographic] texts, concrete action, dialogue, emotion, embodiment, spirituality, and self-consciousness are featured appearing as relational and institutional stories affected by history, social structure and culture..." (2000, p. 739). The manner in which authoethnography is used in this research also connects to BFT as it relates to the field of education in the following ways: (1) it offers the perspective of how sexism and racism intersect in the lives of African American female professors; (2) it offers the experiential knowledge and stories of African American women's experiences as legitimate in teaching about sexism and racial discrimination and in academic institutions; (3) it serves as a means of furthering a social justice agenda as the purpose of this work is to increase institutions' awareness of the experiences of African American female professors in predominantly White institutions in the hope of moving beyond the rhetoric of diversity to the practice of diversity.

Data Sources

The data sources for the autoethnographies stem from recollections of past events (as we remember them), artifacts and documents. The memories of past events are derived from interactions with university administrators, colleagues, staff (including conferences, meetings, colloquiums and other informal conversations) and students (both in class and in informal exchanges during advising sessions, etc.) The documents include personal journal reflections and emails.

Data Analysis

Carolyn Ellis (2004) discusses thematic analysis as one of three ways in which autoethnographic narratives can be analyzed. According to Ellis, "'thematic analysis' refers to treating stories as data and using analysis to arrive at themes that illuminate the content and hold within or across stories" (p. 196). In this study, thematic analysis was employed to analyze the induction of two African American female professors' into the academy. These autoethnographic narratives follow in chapters two and three. They are thematically based as they focus on the themes that emerged from the data.

References

Alex-Assensoh, Y. (2003). Race in the academy: Moving beyond diversity and toward the incorporation of faculty of color in predominately White colleges and universities. *Journal of Black Studies, 34(1)*, 5–11.

Cole J. B. & Guy-Sheftall, B. (2003). *Gender talk: The struggle for women's equality in African American communities.* New York: One World Ballantine Books.

Collins, P.H. (2000). *Black feminist thought: Knowledge, consciousness,and the politics of empowerment.* New York: Routledge.

Dillard, C. (2006). *On spiritual strivings: Transforming an African American woman's academic life.* New York: SUNY.

Dixon-Reeves, R. (2003). Mentoring as a precursor to incorporation: An assessment of the mentoring experience of recently minted Ph.D.s. *Journal of Black Studies, 34(1)*, 12–27.

Ellis, C. (2004). *The ethnographic I: A methodological novel about autoethnography.* Walnut Creek, CA: AltaMira Press.

Ellis C. & Bochner, A.P. (2000). Autoethnography, personal narrative, reflexivity: Researcher as subject. In N.K. Denzin and Y.S. Lincoln (Eds.), *Handbook of qualitative research* (pp. 733–768). Thousand Oaks, CA: Sage.

Essien, V. (2003). Visible and invisible barriers to the incorporation of faculty of color in predominantly White law schools. *Journal of Black Studies*, 34(1), 63–71.

Fenelon, J. (2003). Race, research, and tenure: Institutional credibility and the incorporation of African, Latino, and American Indian faculty. *Journal of Black Studies*, 34(1), 87–100.

Guy-Sheftall, B. (1995). *Words of fire: An anthology of African American feminist thought.* New York: New Press.

Guy-Sheftall, B. (2003). African American Women: The legacy of

Black feminism. In R. Morgan (Ed.) *Sisterhood is forever: The women's anthology for a new millennium* (pp. 176–187) New York: Washington Square Press, 2003.

hooks, b. (1989). *Talking back: Thinking feminist, thinking Black.* Boston: South End Press.

Jarrett-Macauley, D., ed. (1996). *Reconstructing womanhood, reconstructing feminism: Writings on Black women.* New York: Routledge.

Journal of Blacks in Higher Education. (2007). The snail-like progress of Blacks into faculty ranks of higher education. *Journal of Blacks in Higher Education.* Retrieved March 10, 2008, from http://www.jbhe.com/news_views/54_black-facultyprogress.html

Ladson-Billings, G. (2005). *Beyond the big house: African American educators on teacher education.* New York: Teachers College Press.

Lorde, A. (1984). *Sister outsider.* Trumansberg, NY: Crossing Press.

Myers, S. L. J., & Turner, C. S. V. (2001). Affirmative action retrenchment and labor market outcomes for African-American faculty. In B. Lindsay & M. J. Justiz (Eds.), *The quest for equity in higher education: Toward new paradigms in an evolving affirmative action era* (pp. 63–98). Albany, NY: State University of New York Press.

Myers, S. L. & Wilkins, R. (1995). *Minority faculty development project.* Minneapolis, MN: Midwestern Higher Education Commission. (ERIC Document Reproduction Service No. ED 390354)

Norrell, S.A., & Gill, J.I. (1991). *Bringing into focus the factors affecting faculty supply and demand: A primer for higher education and state policy makers.* Boulder, CO: Western Interstate Commission for Higher Education. (ERIC Document Reproduction Service No. ED 370471).

Omolade, B. (1994). *The rising song of African American women.* New York: Routledge.

Ottinger, C., Sikula, R., & Washington, C. (1993). Production of minority doctorates. *Research Briefs*, 4(8). Washington, DC: Division of Policy Analysis and Research, American Council on Education.

Oyewumi, O. (2003). *African women & feminism: Reflecting on the politics of sisterhood.* Trenton, N.J.: Africa World Press.

Schuster, J.H. (1992). Academic labor markets. In B.R. Clark & G.R. Neave (Eds.), *The encyclopedia of higher education, 3* (pp. 1537–1547). Oxford: Pergamon Press.

Smith, D.G., Turner, C.S.V., Osefi-Kofi, N., & Richards, S. (2004). Interrupting the usual: Successful strategies for hiring diverse faculty. *The Journal of Higher Education, 75*(2), 133–160.

Solórzano, D.G. (1993). *The road to the doctorate for California's Chicanas and Chicanos: A study of Ford Foundation minority fellows.* Berkeley: The Regents of the University of California. (ERIC Document Reproduction Service No. ED 374941).

Steady, F.C. (1999). *The Black woman cross-culturally.* Rochester, VT: Schenkman Books, Inc.

Tack, M., & Patitu, C.L. (1992). *Faculty job satisfaction: Women and minorities in peril* (ASHE-ERIC Higher Education Report No. 4). Washington, DC: The George Washington University School of Education and Human Development.

Terborg-Penn, R. & Rushing, A.B. (1996). *Women in Africa and the African diaspora.* Washington, D.C.: Howard University Press.

Thomas, G.D., & Hollenshead, C. (2001). Resisting from the margins: The coping strategies of Black women and other women of color faculty members at a research university. *Journal of Negro Education, 70*(3), 166–175.

Turner, C. S. V. (2000). New faces, new knowledge: As women and minorities join the faculty, they bring intellectual diversity in pedagogy and in scholarship. *Academe, 86*(5), 34-37.

Turner, C.S. (2003). Incorporation and marginalization in the academy: From order toward center for faculty of color? *Journal of Black Studies, 34*(1), 112–125.

Vargas, L. (Ed.) (2002). *Women faculty of color in the White classroom: Narratives on the pedagogical implications of teacher diversity.* New York: Peter Lang Publishing.

CHAPTER TWO

"My Soul Looks Back and Wonders, How I Got Over":
Experiences of a Tenure-Track Neophyte

Cynthia Cole Robinson

> How I got over,
> How did I make it over,
> You know my soul looks back and wonders
> How did I make it over.
>
> Soon as I can see Jesus,
> The Man that made me free,
> The Man that bled and suffered,
> And died for you and me.
>
> I thank Him because He taught me,
> I thank Him because He brought me,
> I thank Him because He kept me,
> Thank Him 'cause He never left me.

(Ward, 1951).

Hiring

It is a warm, balmy morning in July and the heat of the day is promising to be brutal. I get in my car headed east, squinting as the sun pierces through my sunglasses. I soon pull over to take off my suit coat, because the heat is relentless and I have an hour drive. I don't want to rumple my suit because I want to appear polished and intact for my interview for an assistant professorship. I get back into my car and put on The Sounds of Blackness' "The Optimistic," a familiar tune that I always play when I need encouragement and inspiration, and boy am I gonna need it today; my stomach is in knots as I visualize my morning-long job talk at the university in front of a search committee of eight people.

As I drive, I ponder what I will say or what they are expecting to hear. I worry about how they will respond to my research presentation about female dropouts who turn to prostitution in the midst of a lack of education credentials and job training. I remember how often people question me about why I do such research and if it relates to my life experience, which it doesn't, but there is an assumption that the only motives for conducting research on marginalized or disenfranchised groups are personal gain, discovery or reflection (Ivers, Goodvin, Hayes, Zolnikov, 2002). Then I calm myself thinking, you got a university fellowship for this research, people respect what this work has to offer. But still, I wonder about how more conservative members of the committee might receive it. After this pep talk, I decide to just be myself. I don't want a job that I got pretending to be something I'm not because I won't be able to keep that front up. It'll be too painful. If they don't accept me for me, then it's not for me. I feel resolved and assured in my decision to be my unadulterated self.

As I wait in the hall adjusting myself and trying not to sweat, it has to be eighty degrees or more in this un-air-conditioned hallway on the university's oldest campus, oddly enough I feel calm.

"Okay, Cynthia we're ready for you," the tall, tanned, cheerful guy says extending his hand to me. "I'm Russ, we talked on the phone."

I immediately feel at ease, as I remember my hour-long talk with him that felt so much like talking to a kindred spirit. I enter the conference room, taking in the majesty of it. The mahogany table and walls are so stately compared to the rest of the building. It's air conditioned and I am relieved.

I begin my talk with a vignette that describes how I came to my research. As I look up, I can see that they are with me, they are getting it. I see a couple of faces that hold a perplexed look, but I'm not rattled. Reading those words reminds me that it's not about what these people think, I believe in this work and that's enough for me.

As I finish my presentation, I feel pleased because I've been true to myself and this work. I need this job, but I feel like even if I don't get it, somehow things will be alright—God will provide. In my mind I repeat a bible verse that I often meditate on in time of trouble, "For I know the plans I have for you," declares the Lord, "plans to prosper you and not to harm you, plans to give you hope and a future" (Jeremiah 29:10, King James Version).

"I can take questions now," I announce as I wrap up the presentation portion of the talk. They immediately begin to ask questions about who I am, my background and further motivations for my research and I answer honestly. "I grew up on the South Side of Chicago in a family-oriented community that was working to middle class that took a socioeconomic downturn when crack cocaine was introduced to my neighborhood. Out of five girls on my block, I was the only one not to become a teenage mother or a high school dropout so this work grows out of the pain and concern that emerges from my friends' (whom I have to this day) experience as dropouts (though not prostitutes) with very limited job options. They suffer the realities of what it means to be a single mother without a high school diploma."

Suddenly the room is alive with authentic conversation and ponderings. After a series of questions they ask me, "Do you have any questions for us?"

Since there is an air of frankness in the room, I go there, "Yes I do, you've heard my research presentation and let's be honest, I'm not a traditional researcher studying "safe, feel good" topics, so do you see a place for me here considering my research agenda? In other words, will I be the pink elephant or token hire because I have no interest in being that."[1] I'm even in awe of the words that just came out of my mouth.

"Oh no," they assure me and go on to explain the social justice roots of the institution and so on. After my questions, Russ tells me I can leave the room for a break.

After a while, he comes out again and asks me to re-join the group. As I take my seat he says, "You know, we're not going to be coy. This is unusual, but we think we should tell you now that we would love to hire you."

And that was the beginning of my journey in academia. A couple of weeks later, I meet with the dean after I had been recommended for hire by the search committee, and she shares her vision for the college with me (she had only been the dean for three months at this point). "Some people think that research doesn't matter that much here, since it's a teaching institution and all. They'll have you believe that, but I plan to place a new focus on scholarship. That's one of the reasons I'm hiring you, your research agenda. I think new Ph.D.s with a passion for research are just what this college needs. I'll stay on top of you to make sure that you finish your dissertation and I believe you will. Because of that, I feel fine hiring you on the tenure track, but you only have until the end of this year to complete and defend your dissertation."

When she calls to officially offer me the position, she offers me a salary that is less than what I made when I was a high school teacher, but I take it because I need the job and have no clue about how to negotiate salary. I know in my gut that I feel I am being underpaid but because I know assistant professors are poorly paid, I figure I'll accept it to get my foot in the door. This is the beginning of what I would find out later was a huge injustice.

The dean is true to her word. She frequently leaves grant applications in my mailbox and personally emails me to assess where I am in the process. And like a proud parent, she congratulates me when I successfully defend my dissertation that February. That's what I remember most about my first dean, her support and belief in scholarship. I heed her words regarding scholarship and they turn out to be my salvation in the end. She was escorted out of her office the summer after my first year and never returned. I never had a chance to say goodbye. This was the first administrative change, one of what would be many during my time at the university.

Perceptions/Receptions to the University

"Hey honey, can I help you with something?" the woman asks as I approach the copying machine with an armful of syllabi and handouts to copy. "Are you a student worker because students can't use this copying machine; you have to use the one in the library."

I turn to look at her with my cheeks flaming with a mix between anger and embarrassment, "I'm sorry, we haven't met, my name is Cynthia Robinson and I'm a new professor."

I see the embarrassment on her face as she explains, "I'm so sorry, you look so young. I didn't know. I'm Sandy. I just didn't know, students are always using this machine and jamming it up."

I continue on my quest for copies, feeling a bit awkward and wondering if it was because I was young that she made that assumption or because I was Black, as all of the support staff for the college were young Black female workers. It is rare that African American women occupy the ranks of faculty, as most are in service positions in the academy (Malveaux, 2005). I decide that I will try to always look older, wear my glasses and dress in suits to make it more apparent that I am a professor. But it didn't help much, people were always surprised—my students were no exception. Some would go as far as to guess how old I was, to which I responded by saying, "I've been in the field of education for over seven years." Soon I got used to it and it didn't bother me anymore, and when people remarked on how young I looked, I replied, "I hope you still say the same thing fifteen years from now."

Life in the Institution

I was the only person of color in my department. Many researchers report sole minority faculty members as feeling alienated (Patitu & Hinton, 2003; Thomas & Hollenshead, 2001), but that was not my experience. I felt comfortable with my colleagues. We had the kind of department where people spoke their minds and where the chair challenged the institution on social justice issues. She, a veteran of the university, had been tenured many years ago and was one of the most respected faculty members in the university and in her field. She was very supportive of my research and my overall thriving at the university. Though she was very busy, I always felt that I could contact her if I needed her. She had an open door policy and was quick to respond whenever I reached out to her.

My first year in the department (under her leadership—she was the first of three department chairs during my four years at the university), Colleen explained that she rotated the teaching load in the department so that every year or so faculty could teach one heavy term of classes and one light term so that we could focus on scholarship during that term. As I spent time in the university, I grew to learn how novel an opportunity this was. She scheduled me to teach only one class that winter term, and it was the best thing that could have happened to me. I spent that term working on a book proposal. The proposal was accepted and the book was published.[2] Colleen definitely believed in scholarship and saw that the inability to do research would soon fizzle out any passion for teaching and service as she believed that they should be interrelated.

The honeymoon was short lived as we had three chairs over the next three years. That next year, the scholarship rotation was brought to a screeching halt, as we began to function more like other departments in the college. The focus became more about staffing courses as our numbers swelled within our program. We had far more students than we could handle in those years. More students meant more money for the university, which meant less time for research and more service work.

Soon, it was all I could do to keep my head above water. I was constantly asked to coordinate alternative programs for our department but often argued against it because I knew it was an overwhelming commitment and counted for little in the tenure process (Turner, 2002). I had heard first-hand accounts from faculty members who served tirelessly as coordinators and committee members, who were denied tenure and/or promotion due to a soft scholarship record. Hence, I also viewed program coordination as a death sentence for junior faculty members who needed to establish a scholarship record. Besides, I saw what program coordination was doing to Pauline. She had been asked to coordinate a program, and it literally drained her physical strength, time and mental energy. She hardly ever had the chance to work on scholarship. The one opportunity that she had to work on scholarship stemmed from a research grant for which we jointly applied that came out of the provost's office.

There were supports in place for scholarship, if one had the time to actually do it. The university offered a research award for up to ten thousand dollars for which Pauline and I applied and were awarded five thousand dollars. Another committee that formed under the leadership of the first dean was the Faculty Development Committee to which I was appointed my first year and chaired for three years. This was a college-wide committee which aimed to provide research grants for faculty members which furthered the university's strategic themes. Though I was allowed to apply for the grants, the irony was that I never had the time to write or conceive of new research projects due to the time commitment required by my teaching and service load. During my last year at the university, my service consisted of advisor to my students, chair of the Faculty Development Committee (which awarded research grants to faculty members and required monitoring the allocation of awarded funds), university strategic planning committee, university academic planning committee, department search committee chair, and program coordinator of one of our alternative certification programs. Though I didn't know it at the time, the experience of piling on service work for faculty of color is often an issue (Turner, 2002).

As new faculty members, we had to attend monthly faculty meetings that were chaired by the associate dean. It served more as a formal check-in than anything else. Late in the year during the spring quarter, he arranged for us to have a meeting which would focus on the tenure and promotion process at the university.

The faculty member that led the meeting was the most senior African American female professor at the university who was also a department chair. I can recall her advising us to collect everything that we did in a box and organize it into teaching, scholarship and service. She admonished us to be avid record keepers as this file would be the backbone of our tenure document. This was the first guidance I had received regarding the explicit expectations for tenure and promotion. While this was the only direct mentoring I received on preparing for promotion and tenure, I now realize that it was more than many new faculty members receive (Butner, Burley, & Marbley, 2000; Dixon-Reeves, 2003; Thomas & Hollenshead, 2001). She shared her personal experiences with racism from students and how the evaluations could impact tenure review. She was very frank and honest and willing to share her nuggets of experience; however, our mentoring relationship was short lived as she passed away later that year. What most struck me was that no official memorial act was offered by the university, though she had served the institution for many years. An email announcement was simply distributed, and the very next week they were preparing to move someone else into her office. I thought to myself, wow, all those years and that's how they honor your work. Soon, an interim chair was put in place—another African American female professor who started at the university with me—and she worked to have a scholarship established in the deceased professor's name.

Diversity

When I was first hired at the university, there were three African American professors in the college. In the year I was hired, three more were as well—Pauline included. All, but one, were women. Also hired with me were two women of Asian descent and one Muslim woman. I was told that the new dean was committed to diversity.

Though I was the only person of color in the department during my first year, the unit was also committed to diversifying the faculty. Over the years, we hired three more African American women of whom one was disabled (I chaired the committee that resulted in the hiring of one), one Latino male, and one male who self-identified as gay. Though we wanted to hire diverse faculty, search chairs said that they did not know where to advertise to attract them. I suggested some advertising outlets when I was chair that seemed to result in more diverse applicants. I would submit that *hiring* diverse faculty wasn't the issue at my institution, *retention* was.[3] One person left due to an overwhelming service load, the requirement to teach at various campuses which resulted in long commuting times and friction with the chair. Another was asked to leave due to work-related issues. Of the faculty of color hired in the college during my time there, fifty percent left. I sometimes jokingly refer to it as the exodus. Many of those who remain express some of the same issues. In a focus group of diverse faculty, though I was not invited to participate, I was told that of the participants present none responded "yes" to the question that asked if they saw themselves remaining at the institution. Hence, I would say that the problem definitely centered more on retention than hiring. This focus group on diversity took place during my last year so I do not know what diversity initiatives might have emerged from this data.

During my time in my department, I frequently voiced concerns over my students' (over 98% White in most of my classes) lack of experience and sometimes stereotypical views of diversity as it related to race, class and gender, a theme echoed by many scholars in the field (Vargas, 2002). The first day of class would prove to be interesting as I would read puzzled looks on students' faces when they realized that I was the professor.

This look was once confirmed during a conversation with one of my Asian American male students, "Dr. Robinson, I have been thinking about the readings we are doing on education and I think that I would like to teach in an African American school on the South Side, but I'm scared about how I will be perceived by the students. You know I used to operate the "El" (public transit train) on the South Side, and the students would often make fun of my accent. Also, there are so many negative stereotypes of Asians in the African American community."

"I can relate to what you're saying, I have that experience all the time as an African American teaching in a predominantly White field, students really look perplexed when they find out that I'm the professor.[4]"

"Yeah, but as soon as you open your mouth in the first five minutes they know you're the real deal," he says.

I want to know more about what he means by that but don't go further into it since I am trying to address his concern. However, I assume he is talking about the language issue as I speak Standard English without an accent in my classes. I think that he is focusing on the language accent issue since that was what he referred to when we first started to talk.[5]

"You can't let that stop you from doing something you have a passion for. There will always be people who hold stereotypical views. Just like you said about students 'knowing I'm the real deal' when your students see that you really care, they'll know that you are too. That's what's important to students. They love, respect and are willing to learn from teachers who really care and embrace them," I add.

Other members of the department voiced their concern for students' views and lack of experience with diversity as well. This was of particular concern as many would be teaching in urban areas some day. As a result, we decided that a new course on urban education was needed. The diversity issues focused on in the class were race, ethnicity, gender, special needs, class and sexual orientation. I, along with another colleague, developed the course. In the end, the course was approved and became a requirement for our program. While this was definitely a sign of progress, segregating diversity into special classes gives the impression that diversity is a "pit stop" experience and not anything to be woven throughout one's life, understanding and interaction with society (Vargas, 2002). I would hope that issues of diversity would become integrated throughout all coursework.

Lessons Learned, Decisions Made

"Cynthia, do you have any concerns or anything you'd like to share with me, how are things going?" the associate dean asks as we sat in my office. This was my annual review and he was conducting it instead of the department chair, as the new chair was not tenured (nor would her successor be).

"Yes," I answer. "I am concerned about two issues in particular: my salary—I feel that I am being underpaid—and the conflict between service and scholarship. For one, I received an email with the average salaries for the college and the university compared to similar institutions and I am being underpaid." I was greatly affected by this and was upset that I had become a part of the statistic of overworked and underpaid women of color professors (Gregory, 2001; Guillory, 2001). He promises to look into it, but nothing comes out of it.

As far as the scholarship is concerned he replies, "I want to urge you to continue to make time for research and writing, though this is a teaching institution. You are early in your career and you want to be sure to continue to establish yourself. I want you to stay here, would love to have you but if you ever want to go to another institution, more emphasis will be placed on your scholarship. My advice is that you still work to perform as though you were at a research institution." This was his advice and he shared it on at least two other occasions. I think it was definitely some of the best mentoring advice that I received as he showed an interest in my overall career development as an academic as opposed to a faculty member at our particular institution.

Though it was extremely difficult to do so, I was able to work on scholarship and had a book published. When my fourth and final department chair took leadership (he was also a tenure track assistant professor), my book was under contract. He told me, "Now that you have the book, you should be fine as far as scholarship in the tenure and promotion process."

This was a great concern to me, it seemed as though the book was a double-edged sword. While it was beneficial for scholarship purposes, it now seemed as though the thought was that now I didn't need as much time for research. Considering that he had yet to go through the tenure and promotion process himself, I was not convinced that I could now turn my focus away from scholarship. I needed to work on peer-reviewed journal publications as well. I remembered the advice of my first dean and the associate dean. I felt as though a moratorium had been placed on my research agenda. Soon my thoughts seemed to be confirmed.

"Cynthia, I need you to coordinate one of the alternative certification programs. We really don't have anyone else that can do it," he said. This was a familiar request and battle I had fought over the years—refusing the program coordination role. Though I had successfully been able to make the argument in the past because of my need to work on scholarship, it was difficult to make the argument as I had just published the book and he thought that was sufficient for scholarship. Also, over the past two years we had a fifty percent attrition rate which led to me being one of the senior faculty members in the department though I had been there for only three years at that point.

I felt a tightness rise in my chest as I answered, "Okay, if you don't have anyone else. You know that I don't think that it's a good idea to put a tenure track person in this role as it takes too much time away from scholarship, but I feel like I'm caught between a rock and a hard place." Prior to becoming chair, he agreed with my position. However, he worked directly against it in his role as chair. I left that day feeling like I was entering a black hole of sorts—I could forget about doing any more research. Also, at this point I was chairing two committees and serving on two others. To add to that, nothing had been done about my salary.

That weekend, I talked with Pauline (she had left the university almost two terms ago), and she lamented that I was now being put in the role that had stunted her own research agenda and drained her energy. That following Monday, I called my chair. "Stan, I've re-thought things and you know what, I've decided that I am not going to serve as the coordinator. It adds too much work to my already heavy workload for which I'm being underpaid. People who do less and are not even tenure track or Ph.D.s make more money than me. I just can't go along with this."

"I'm going to talk to the dean about this. If I can get them to adjust your salary, will you head the program?" he asked.

"I don't know; let's just see what happens and we'll talk about that then." However, as I thought about it I saw what he was propos-ing as ridiculous. Why should I have to do more work in order to get paid what I should have been paid in the first place?

This negotiation process took forever. Soon he brought in Colleen who was still a member in the department. She called me one day as I lay in bed despondent with despair and pondering what my next steps should be, 'should I leave? Will they never right this wrong? "Cynthia, this is Colleen. Stan told me what was going on with your salary. I can't believe they're still pulling this kind of stuff. Do you think it's racial? Because I think it's more gender.[6] They did that to me years ago; they were paying the men more."

"You know what Colleen, I really don't think that the EEOC is gonna split that hair," I answered with what little energy I had left.

"It makes me so angry. I talked with an administrator about it and she's going to work on it. She sees your position," she said.

When I hung up the phone with her that evening, tears were roll-ing down my face. I felt some relief, like something finally was going to be done. Colleen appealed to her on the basis of gender equity, something to which most women in our field can relate. However, as an African American woman experiencing double oppression (Collins, 2000), it was very difficult to determine what kind of dis-crimination it was and as far as I was concerned, both were equally as damaging, wrong and hurtful. The dean kept to her word and the provost, also a woman, agreed to adjust my salary. However while she was away on vacation, the vice provost (a man) rejected the increase. Devastation. Despair. Anger. I couldn't believe it. At this point I knew I was up against something very deep. I felt renewed in my quest to have this righted.

During this time, new contracts were coming out, and the deadline for re-signing for the next year was swiftly approaching, so I called my dean to see what I should do with this contract that still reflected my current rate. She advised me to sign with an explanation of where we were in the process and what my expectations were of the outcome. I complied. A short time later, I received a call from the dean, it had been taken care of. I was finally going to be paid on par. The victory was bittersweet; I had the desired outcome (though not back pay) but was battle worn and weary.

During my last week at the university, after I had been hired by my current institution, I was approached by an African American male faculty member who had some concerns about his salary. He wanted to know if he should be making more. He shared the salary at which he was brought into the university and it was twenty percent more than my incoming salary; he was also hired All But Dissertation (A.B.D). I was floored. This made me reconsider what Colleen had told me about gender discrimination.

The workload, overwhelming service, the fight to find time to do research and write combined with the unequal pay saga finally had taken its toll. I decided to leave, not in search of a perfect place, but a place where I could be treated more equitably and supported by a reasonable balance of teaching, service and scholarship.

Notes

1 Dominguez (1994) speaks of the notion of the minority as "exotic other."

2 *From the Classroom to the Corner: Female Dropouts' Reflections on Their School Years (2007).*

3 For more on issues of retaining faculty of color, see Weems (2003) and Turner (2002).

4 Female professors of color experiences of White students' initial reactions to their role as instructor are frequently documented in Vargas' edited volume, *Women Faculty of Color in the White Classroom.*

5 Delpit (2006) discusses the need to speak the language of the "culture of power."

References

Butner, B.K., Burley, H. & Marbley, A.F. (2000). Coping with the unexpected: Black faculty at predominately White institutions. *Journal of Black Studies, 30*(3), 453–462.

Collins, P.H. (2000). *Black feminist thought.* New York: Routledge.

Delpit, L. (2006). *Other people's children: Cultural conflict in the classroom.* New York: The New Press.

Dixon-Reeves, R. (2003). Mentoring as a precursor to incorporation: An assessment of the mentoring experience of recently minted Ph.D.s. *Journal of Black Studies, 34*(1), 12–27.

Dominguez, V. (1994). A taste for 'the other': Intellectual complicity in racializing practices. *Current Anthropology, 35*(4): 333–348.

Gregory, S.T. (2001). Black faculty women in the academy: History, status and future. *Journal of Negro Education, 70*(3), 124–138.

Guillory, E.A. (2001). The Black professoriate: Explaining the salary gap for African-American female professors. *Race, Ethnicity and Education,* 4(3), 225–244.

Ivers, S., Goodvin, R., Hayes, S. & Zolnikov, B. (2002, June). *Minor concerns: An exploration of the objectives and issues of minority research.* Paper presented at People of Color in Predominantly White

Institutions Conference. Retrieved June 18, 2009, from http://www.digitalcommons.unl.edu/cgi/viewcontent.cgi?article= 1025.

Malveaux, J. (2005, April 7). Nurturer or queen bee? *Diverse Issues in Higher Education*, Article 4461. Retrieved June 19, 2009, from http://www.diverseeducation.com/artman/publish/article4461.ht ml.

Patitu, C. L., & Hinton, K. G. (2003, Winter). The experiences of African American women faculty and administrators in higher education: Has anything changed? In M. F. Howard-Hamilton (Ed.), *New directions for student services. Meeting the needs of African American women* (pp. 79–93). San Francisco: Jossey-Bass.

Robinson, C.C. (2007). *From the classroom to the corner: Female dropouts' reflections on their school years*. New York: Peter Lang.

Thomas, G.D. & Hollenshead, C. (2001). Resisting from the margins: The coping strategies of Black women and other women of color faculty members at a research university. *The Journal of Negro Education*, *70*(3), 166–175.

Turner, C.S.V. (2002). Women of color in academe: Living with multiple marginality. *The Journal of Higher Education*, *73*(1), 74–93.

Vargas, L. (2002). Women faculty of color in the White classroom. New York: Peter Lang.

Ward, C. (1951). How I got over. Newark, NJ: Savoy Records.

Weems, R.E. (2003). The incorporation of Black faculty at predominantly White institutions: A historical and contemporary perspective. *Journal of Black studies*, *34*(1), 101–111.

CHAPTER THREE

"Amazing Grace":
Examining One Woman's Induction into the Academy

Pauline Clardy

> Amazing grace, how sweet the sound
> That saved a wretch like me!
> I once was lost, but now am found,
> Was blind, but now I see.
>
> 'Twas grace that taught my heart to fear,
> And grace my fears relieved;
> How precious did that grace appear,
> The hour I first believed!
>
> ...Through many dangers, toils and snares,
> I have already come;
> 'Tis grace has brought me safe thus far,
> And grace will lead me home...

Excerpt from "Amazing Grace" (Newton, 1779)

The Hiring Process

The American Educational Research Association's (AERA) annual meeting took place in my home town that year, and for the first time as a graduate student, I included my vita in the AERA Career Center because I was finishing my dissertation and I knew that I would soon need employment. Representatives from interested universities left messages for me and I followed up with each of them even though I knew that I had to work locally to continue to care for an elderly parent who was ill. One institution from the area left a message for me to schedule an interview which I made several attempts to do, but I was unsuccessful in contacting them for two months. It was not until I finally gave up hope that someone returned my calls. By that time, Cynthia had been hired by this school, and she had told me about her interview experience, so I was excited to finally hear from someone. I had two other friends, both White males, who had been hired the year before and by that time occupied positions of authority in the university. One had finished his doctoral degree the previous year and had been made chair of the doctoral program.

The coordinator of the program for which I applied contacted me and invited me to present my research before a panel of faculty members. She also told me that I would be treated to lunch following the presentation so that I could interact with the faculty in a less formal atmosphere. It was already summer by then and many of the faculty members were on vacation. That is why when I walked into the room where I was to present my research and only three faculty members were there to greet me, I did not find it unusual that more faculty had not come. Among those present was the program coordinator, another faculty member from the department and a professor from a different department.

As I presented my dissertation which was still a work in progress albeit in the final stages, I tried to gauge the panel's interest. The professor from a different department fell asleep during the presentation, but the program coordinator and the faculty member from the department appeared to take an interest in what I was presenting. Afterwards, they gave me comments on the research and encouraged me because they knew that my defense date was quickly approaching. Before I left, there was some discussion among the faculty members as to whether we would go to lunch, but in the end, it was decided that due to other appointments that they had, we would forgo this part of the process. The program coordinator then told me that she wanted me to meet with the department chair and the dean on the following day at the downtown campus. I thanked them for their time and left.

The next day, I met both the department chair and the dean in separate meetings. Both of them greeted me enthusiastically and told me that they were impressed with my credentials and wanted to hire me. I was initially excited until they offered me several thousand dollars less than I had made as a graduate student. Cynthia had told me the salary that she had been offered, stating that she did not negotiate for more because she was a new assistant professor. I negotiated for more because I thought that my years of experience in academia should count for something even though I had never been an assistant professor before. They offered me $2,000 more and told me that the amount was as high as they could go. Reluctantly, I accepted the offer because by that point, I simply needed a job.

The dean told me that she was new in her position and that she wanted to make changes in the institution which had been known as a teachers' college. One change that she wanted to make was to encourage and support research. She told me that she liked my research because of its social justice orientation. The dean also advised me to "protect" myself from service overload and concentrate on scholarship and teaching. Regrettably, the institution did not support the dean's visions and eventually let her go. Before I knew it, I had several service responsibilities and an alternative certification program to coordinate, which I had agreed to do before I was hired, not realizing the amount of time it would require.

First Impressions

The sun was bright on that September morning and the day held many possibilities. This particular day was to be a special one for me—my first official day as an assistant professor in academia. I had gotten my office assignment in the mail, and I was excited to be assigned to the suburban campus near my home. My department chair had told me that she thought I would be a good role model for the students, both Black as well as White, because I represented a positive image of an African American woman in academia. At least she didn't say *You're a credit to your race,* I thought.

My husband, Eugene, and I loaded all of my books, office supplies and personal mementos from friends that celebrated my new title of "Doctor" into our car. When I arrived at the campus, my first surprise was that my office was not in the main building. I showed a security guard the letter that indicated my office assignment, and he pointed me in the direction of a smaller building located in the middle of the parking lot.

"Oh that's where the faculty offices must be," I told Eugene.

As Eugene and I entered the building, we were overwhelmed by a stench that seemed to emanate from a sewer. Directly facing us across from the entrance was a stairwell that had been roped off to the public. A sign stating that the second floor had been condemned was attached to the rope. Believing that I had been pointed in the wrong direction, I started to exit the building. Then I heard someone speak from the next room, "Can I help you?" When Eugene and I entered the room, an older White woman seated at a table going though some boxes grabbed her purse, held it tightly to her chest and looked at me from head to toe. Then she asked us who we were and what we wanted. Her interrogating look made me feel as though not only did she question my identity but she also questioned my right to be there. Sensing her doubt and apprehension, I showed the woman my I.D. and explained that I was the new assistant professor and that I had brought some items that I wanted to leave in my new office.

The woman immediately made a phone call without saying anything to me or my husband. We waited at her desk for someone to come and let us into my office.

Still excited about my new position, I turned to Eugene and said, "I'm sure that's just standard procedure."

He nodded in agreement.

A janitor came and showed the woman where the key to my office was.

In a low voice, she stated, "I know where the keys are. I wasn't expecting her today."

"I guess I should have phoned ahead," I told Eugene.

"Yes, you probably should have," he replied.

The janitor took the key, introduced himself and told us to follow him. Upon reaching my office which was the only one without a name posted on the door, the janitor unlocked the door. My countenance fell as I looked around the room to find what looked like thirty-year-old blinds falling from the window and equally aged wall paper removing itself from walls that bled water and other liquids that I could not identify. Another look around the room revealed cobwebs hanging from the corners of the room.

"As you can see, we weren't quite ready for you," the janitor told me. With the beginning of classes only two days away, I wondered how long it would take for my office to be ready for me to work there.

"Not much will be done to the office, but we will clean it up for you. We plan to move to a better facility someday, hopefully in the next year or two," the janitor stated.

After showing me my new office, the janitor took me on a tour of the campus, which consisted of a main building that used to serve as the county courthouse and that still had jail cells on one of the floors. There were a few offices in the main building but not many. As we walked around the buildings, the janitor told me many humorous stories about the gangsters of yesteryear who had once called the jail home. At the end of our tour, his demeanor changed as he became very serious. The janitor stated, "Come and get me if you ever need to be escorted to your car. These students can be difficult to faculty that [he paused] they don't know." He repeated this several times, which made me feel uncomfortable and made me wonder if I had made the right choice in coming to the school.

By the time classes began, my office had been cleaned and painted. A year later, I was given an office at the downtown campus which was in a modern building. Eventually, the suburban campus to which I was originally assigned closed and relocated to a modern corporate facility in a different suburban location.

Life in the Institution

When I graduated from a research one university, I thought that research would be a major part of what I did as an assistant professor. Not so. Not because I lacked the desire or the ability but because my responsibilities at the school where I worked consumed so much of my time that I could not concentrate on anything other than teaching, coordinating a program, advising and performing service inside and outside of the university.

Furthermore, I never understood the course load assignments at the university. As I saw it, each person in my department taught two classes each quarter. In my case, I taught two classes and coordinated a very dysfunctional alternative certification program. Each faculty member in my department had advisees, but because I also coordinated a program, I advised the students in the program in addition to the regular program students. Over time, I accumulated nearly twice as many advisees as my colleagues.

My program was dysfunctional by nature due to the fact that it was new and that recent changes in state government (which government officials didn't appear to understand) affected the program. Students called or wrote e-mails each day—all day—about their individual employment situations which depended on their successful enrollment in the program and eventual completion. Each time they took and did not pass a state examination, they would receive a letter threatening their employment, and each time, they asked me to vouch for them to their employers. Some of them lost their jobs and because their employment was required to participate in the alternative certification program, they pleaded with me to make exceptions for them which I could not do, but I often helped them identify teaching positions to apply for or I used my contacts to get them work so that they could remain in the program. It was stressful work which often consumed most of my time. At one point, I had nearly two hundred very needy advisees whom I heard from regularly. Working so closely with the students, I began to bond with them. I did not know that at other schools advisors were assigned to work with students instead of faculty members.

When I met with my department chair, she often spoke about research. She explained that research was important for consideration for tenure. As such, she advised me to take one full day per week to work only on research. I tried to take her advice but found it impossible to do given the nature of the program that I coordinated and the needs of the students in it. As time went on, I learned from colleagues that coordinating the alternative certification program had not been something that they wanted to do. They had planned to "dump" it on the new faculty member because they knew how dysfunctional the program would be and that it would not give them time to do their research. In all of my time at the university, I participated in one research project, which was funded by a faculty development grant that Cynthia and I applied for and received. There were other opportunities for grants to fund research at the university, but there was little time to conduct the research projects.

In the area of mentoring, when the first dean had been there, she scheduled monthly meetings for new faculty members to be mentored. The most valuable of these meetings was a workshop on promotion and tenure. When the dean left, the group eventually stopped meeting. The closest semblance of mentoring other than the meetings was when a colleague came to my first class with me and explained the program requirements to the students. She gave me her telephone number, and each week I called her to get answers to the questions that I had. I was also told that the full professor in my department would answer my questions, which he did.

Becoming an assistant professor was truly a turning point in my life in more ways than one. I had been in education for many years. I even worked in higher education when I was a doctoral student, so the university was not a new venue for me, but the position as a tenure track professor was different than any other that I had held.

For my first quarter, I taught at both the suburban and downtown campuses. There was more diversity in the group of students in the city than in the suburban group. My colleagues had warned me about the group in the suburbs, stating that they might be prejudiced. I found both groups to be accepting of me as their professor once I gave them my syllabus and explained my expectations. One of the assignments that I gave both groups was to spend time in the presence of another ethnic group. The group in the suburbs appeared to be less enthusiastic about the assignment at first, but after the project was done, the comments that they made showed me that they had gotten a great deal out of it. As reported by the students, their reluctance and apprehension about the assignment stemmed from lack of exposure to other groups, but they expressed their gratefulness for the opportunity to go out of their comfort zones to spend time with people from other racial and ethnic groups. After the assignment, at least one third of the students said that they now intend to work with students in areas of high need such as schools that African Americans and/or Latinos attend because these groups of students were in dire need of good, dedicated teachers.

Many of my colleagues who were faculty of color at my school and other institutions told me of their plight in university classrooms consisting of a White majority student population. The main problem that they reported was lack of respect from students who challenged their credentials and resisted reading about issues related to cultural and linguistic minorities. I knew that their complaints were valid because many of my students brought their complaints against other faculty of color to me (as if I had any authority in the university structure to address their issues). Personally, I never experienced disrespect from my students. In fact, I formed a bond with many of them that continues to this day. In all honesty, I can say that I care about each of my students, and our work together feeds my spirit. As reported by students in their reviews of my classes, they acknowledged and appreciated the effort and expertise that I put into my work. I view education as my vocation, and I strive hard to put forth my best possible effort.

Diversity

"Diversity." "Social Justice." These were terms that people mentioned in passing and even in some meetings, but there were few initiatives that addressed diversity while I was employed at the university. Of those few, there were initiatives that aimed at bringing more Latino students into the school, which had an overwhelming majority of White students. The alternative certification program that I coordinated was open to all students, regardless of race or ethnicity; however, it attracted minorities who were already teaching but did not have teaching certificates. One of the problems with the program was that it lacked the infrastructure to support these students, many of whom had been products of sub-standard schooling. My attempts to provide resources for them were denied by the administration.

To my knowledge, there were no initiatives to recruit faculty of color after the dean was forced out, and little diversity among the faculty in terms of race or ethnicity. More importantly, there were no persons of color in the administration. An African American colleague of mine formed a diversity committee which I joined, but the committee met only one time and then stopped meeting. The purpose of this committee was never clearly articulated.

In terms of educating the students how to teach in a diverse society, diversity was addressed through the Interstate New Teacher Assessment and Support Consortium (INTASC) and the Illinois Professional Teaching Standards (IL-PTS) for students in the Elementary Education Program in one category of their online portfolio, i.e., Individual Student Need. I reviewed hundreds of portfolios and, in addressing these standards, most of my students did not enter artifacts that dealt with racial, cultural or gender diversity. At the time, cultural diversity was only infused in coursework on multicultural education, bilingual education and later urban studies.

Whenever diversity was mentioned in a meeting that I attended, faculty deferred to me or another person of color to address the issue. While at this university, I received requests to speak to classes about diversity at my institution as well as others in the area. Was it the color of my skin that qualified me as an expert on the topic? Accepting the charge, I began to read voraciously on diversity and multicultural education. I accepted all invitations because as I saw it, the teaching population continued to be mainly White and female while the student population was becoming more culturally and linguistically diverse. I wanted to do what I could to help future teachers understand how to address the needs and interests of diverse student populations.

As an African American, I am automatically considered a minority in this society. Every since I was a freshman in high school, I have been a minority within school settings. That is why being a minority at the university was nothing new for me. Another colleague of mine had been born in Colombia (I am using Colombia for the sake of anonymity), so for her being a minority in a majority White university in the United States was a new experience. One day, while in a department meeting, this colleague spoke out on diversity. The two of us were the only people of color in attendance at this meeting.

"I have held this in for too long. I have to say something." The room became quiet as my Colombian colleague spoke.

"There are some issues that we need to discuss but we never include these in our meetings." The more she spoke, the more emotional she became.

"Why aren't we discussing diversity here? I have some issues as a person of color that never get addressed." Faces of some faculty members turned red as she spoke, but no one else said anything.

"Why is it that my research about children of color isn't supported?" She continued as she posed several questions that must have been viewed as rhetorical because no one answered.

"Why is my voice not given the same consideration as that of others in the department? What does a person of color have to do in this department to become a part of the club? I see collegiality all of the time but I'm not included," she continued nearly at the point of tears. As she spoke, our colleagues, almost in unison, changed their gaze from my Colombian counterpart to me. I assume for a reaction.

Everyone in the department was pleasant. I saw collegiality amongst my department members but, like my Colombian colleague, I never felt like a part of the group either. As well, I witnessed White people coming to our department and quickly being accepted among the faculty even to the point that their telephone numbers were stored in the "contacts" of the cell phones of other faculty in the department. I also heard them talking about things that they did together outside of work, but I was seldom invited to take part in their extracurricular activities.

As the only other person of color, I wanted to chime in and support my Colombian colleague because no one else was saying anything. I did not want to leave her out on a limb, so to speak, but I had enjoyed my invisibility and space on the margin for so long that I felt uncomfortable relinquishing it even for a moment. I recalled the words of bell hooks:

> I am located on the margin. I make a definite distinction between the marginality which is imposed by oppressive structures and that marginality one chooses as a site of resistance—as location of radical openness and possibility. (hooks, 1990, p. 153)

"I understand what you're saying," I finally managed to utter as I spoke out for the first time in a department meeting. "I also feel alone and unsupported here," I said. The conversation between my Colombian colleague and I continued. It was a definite switch. Usually, everyone else spoke out in the meetings and we remained silent. The more I spoke, the more empowered I felt. Then the person with the highest rank in the department, a White male full professor, made a statement that ended the meeting and all future dialogues about diversity:

"Okay. Now, I hope the two of you feel better. That is all of the bitching and moaning that is going to be tolerated."

Lessons Learned, Decisions Made

One thing that I noticed about this university was that it was run more like a business than a school. They attracted excellent professors, so I believe that the students received a quality education; however, the programs were accelerated to the point that I often wondered how well prepared the students could be. Case in point: teacher candidates completed their student teaching in ten weeks. At my current university, students participate in a year-long internship which enables them to see what teachers experience from the beginning of a school year to its completion. Which group of students would a principal be more likely to hire?

The university also was known to create programs without much research or preparation. An opportunity would arise and the university would run with it, assigning faculty members to coordinate these ventures that were laden with "administrivia" instead of hiring non tenure track program coordinators, which would have been helpful in protecting the time of tenure track faculty who were expected to produce scholarship. Even though I already coordinated one such program, my department chair approached me and asked me to consider taking on an additional one. I later learned that she had asked others in the department but they had refused. I told her that I could not take on the additional responsibility in light of everything else that I was doing. I knew that this additional program would require so much of my already limited time that I would never be able to produce any research. Later, Cynthia told me that in a conversation that she had with my department chair in passing, the woman told her that she planned to convince me to coordinate the new program.

By year three, I had consistently worked hard and received excellent reports of my teaching even though I was dealing with a situation at home that required much of my time and energy—taking care of my elderly mother. I was determined not to allow my home responsibilities to interfere with my work at the university, and it never did. I paid nurses to attend to my mother while I worked and I took care of her after work often without getting much sleep. The price that I paid is that at the end of each school year, I literally collapsed from exhaustion and ended up in a cardiac ward.

During the winter quarter of year three when I received my course load assignment, I realized that I could not take it any longer. My department chair said that I would teach two classes, facilitate a seminar and supervise nine student teachers and practicum students as well as coordinate the alternative certification program and possibly a new one. I would also be expected to produce scholarship, but none of this would be considered overload, so I would not receive any additional compensation. I didn't understand how this was equitable nor did I understand certain other practices of the university. Case in point: I still do not understand the university's explanation of why our W2 income tax statements showed several thousand dollars less than the salary amount that appeared on our contracts as our total yearly income. The low salary barely covered my living expenses, and with the added responsibility of paying for eldercare for my mother, I was nearly destitute.

Finally, I realized that I could not thrive in an institution such as this, and tenure would be nearly impossible to attain in spite of the exorbitant amount of time I spent completing my assigned duties for the university. To leave was a difficult decision to make given the ties that I had made with my students and the spiritual enrichment that I had gotten as a result of our work together. But in the end, I left. I vividly remember telling Cynthia in one of our many conversations, "Girl, that is it for me. I'd rather return to the elementary school classroom [which I loved] than to stay here. At least I'd be able to afford groceries on a consistent basis and get some much-needed rest every now and then."

Making Meaning of My Experiences

The data for this research have been presented thematically, and I will base my meaning-making on the themes that emerged as they relate to: 1) increasing institutions' awareness of how women faculty of color experience life within the academy which can aid in institutional efforts to attract and retain members of this group, and 2) creating a dialogue and developing support networks for women faculty members of color who may have similar experiences. I in no way believe that I can speak for all women of color or that my experiences represent those of every person of color. Also, due to the nature of qualitative research, it is not my intention to generalize (Creswell, 2007). It is my hope that my experiences can be informative and enlightening whether to university officials who enact diversity policies or recruit faculty of color or to faculty of color who teach in predominantly White universities.

First, no one, regardless of race, should have been received with the disrespect that I was given, beginning with the search committee and onsite personnel. I tried to be objective and look beyond obvious disrespectful behavior such as one of the faculty members falling asleep during my presentation and the discussion about whether to take me to lunch. Though I tried to mask it, these behaviors and the resulting action (or inaction) made me feel as though they thought my research, which focused on linguistic and cultural minorities, was not important to them and that I was not worth the time or energy of taking me to lunch.

It is not my orientation to "play the race card" or claim that racism is the root of all inequitable treatment, but due to the history of racism that has been and remains present in our society and is reflected in our schools (Ladson-Billings, 2000), it should be obvious why many people of color, particularly African Americans, when faced with inequitable or unfair treatment, often attribute it to race. A special effort to include faculty of color and treat them equitably and with respect is mandatory. Anything else is unacceptable.

Next, I tried to justify the woman's reaction when I reported to my campus to move into my office by thinking that she behaved in this way because she did not expect me, which might have been the case, but the look in her eyes and the clutching of her purse reminded me of similar actions by White women in the building where my husband and I lived when he got on elevators or walked down the hall. Again, racism in the broader society was reflected in the school (Ladson-Billings, 2000).

Reflecting on the condition of the office in a building that should not have been open to the public is still painful. There were White professors with offices in the building, but not one was in the condition that mine was in when I first came to campus two days before classes began. I was taken aback by this but in all honesty I was not alarmed because as a person who has experienced racism her entire life, I had grown accustomed to unfair treatment. Again, disrespect in any form is unacceptable. Institutions must make a concerted effort to prepare for the needs of new faculty if they expect to retain them (Plata, 1996).

While reflecting on these issues, I am reminded of a presentation by Dr. William Smith (2008) of the University of Utah. The topic of Dr. Smith's lecture was "Racial Battle Fatigue among Students of Color: The Campus Racial Environment and African American Males." Although his discussion focused on African American male students, I could equate much of what he talked about to my experiences as an African American female professor. One such concept is that of racial battle fatigue. As I previously mentioned, at the end of each year as an assistant professor, I collapsed and ended up in a cardiac ward. I did not consider manifestations of racism as a contributing factor to my health problems at the time, but as Dr. Smith also pointed out in his speech, racial micro aggressions can be harmful—felt as assaults to the people who receive them. In hindsight, I can see how internalizing disrespectful behaviors might have affected my physical as well as mental health. Another of Smith's salient points was that spirituality is cathartic for African Americans in academia because it helps us deal with the manifestations of racism. What he contended is logical since spirituality has played the same role in the larger society for African Americans since slavery. Spirituality continues to play a major role in my life inside and outside of the academy.

The entire hiring process was new to me, so I did not have anything to compare my experience to until I was interviewed at my current school. The department secretary contacted me and told me that the search committee would very much like to interview me for the position of Bilingual/Bicultural and Multicultural Education Assistant Professor. There was warmth and excitement in her voice, and she made me feel as though the committee thought I was someone special. She then proceeded to give me a choice of dates for a phone interview, explaining how long the process should take. She told me that at least one question would be in Spanish. The search committee was composed of bilingual faculty and staff, elementary education faculty, and graduate students. The morning following the interview, the secretary phoned me again and stated that the search committee was very impressed with my credentials and my interview, so they wanted to invite me to campus to meet with several parties and present my research. Again, she offered me several dates. The department put me up in a nice hotel and had faculty members and students escort me to all meals (breakfast, lunch and dinner each day) in nice restaurants over the three days that I was in town. At each meal, those present informally interviewed me and later provided feedback to the search committee about their impressions of me. I met formally with the bilingual student advocacy group, the associate dean, the department chair, and the promotion and tenure committee which was the only group that did not appear very friendly at first. I think that they wanted to impress upon me the importance of their review process. One of the members asked how I would feel about being given feedback on my progress. I told him that I welcomed the idea because at my previous school, I never received feedback from faculty or the administration, only the students. With that said, the committee welcomed me to the campus and gave me their support. I presented my research to what appeared to be the majority of the faculty; they asked me many questions and showed a great deal of interest. There was a reception held in my honor afterwards and people from departments throughout the building came to meet me. I was also given a tour of the town by a realtor. The experience felt surreal. I recall telling Cynthia later, "Girl, I felt like I was in a fairytale or dream. If it was a dream, I never wanted to wake up from it."

The morning after I returned home, the department chair phoned me. With enthusiasm in her voice she stated, "Dr. Clardy, I would like to extend an offer of employment to you. The entire search committee and everyone who met you agree that you would be an asset to our bilingual education program, department, and college." With that said, she offered me several thousand dollars more than I made at my previous institution, and stated, "I don't believe in offering any one of your background and qualifications anything less than top salary for the position." I accepted immediately.

There is no comparison between the treatment that I received at the first school and the treatment that I enjoy at my current university. It is not my intention to discredit one and build up another because there are issues related to diversity at my current school as well. But rather, my purpose is to show universities the importance of treating all faculty with respect and dignity.

Another important consideration for universities is that junior faculty, regardless of gender, race or ethnicity, should be put in a position where there is support in terms of scholarship, teaching and service (Tack & Patitu, 1992). In order for assistant professors to have a future in academia, they should not have the burden of coordinating a program or an excessive teaching load or service requirement without a proper support system in place; i.e., course release, additional compensation, differentiated load, etc. To avoid attrition, a rule of thumb is never to assign tasks to junior faculty that other faculty members do not want to do. At my first institution, no one else in the department wanted to run the alternative certification program; therefore, I, the new professor, was given this task and later slated to coordinate an additional program. With such responsibility, it would have been difficult, perhaps impossible, to write for publication; therefore, tenure would not have been attainable.

Next, mentoring is of utmost importance, and no junior faculty member should be without an assigned mentor (Dixon-Reeves, 2003) even if they decide to work with a mentor of their choosing instead. At my current university, I was given a mentor but I chose to work with someone else because my mentor was not on my campus and communication was difficult. My self-selected mentor has made a huge difference in my approach to scholarship in particular. As a result, I have been more productive in this area.

Additionally, people of color express that they experience both marginalization and invisibility in majority White institutions (Alfred, 2001; hooks, 1990). Women of color experience marginality in multiple ways (Turner, 2002). Universities must be mindful of this and put forth an effort to include diverse faculty in the same way that White faculty are included whether it is in supporting their research agendas which are often discredited by their White male counterparts (Aguirre, 2000) or including them in minutes from meetings or in activities that take place off campus. Even at my current university, I have noticed that many of my comments have not been reflected in the minutes of meetings. What I like about my current university is that when I am silent in meetings, I am asked what my opinion is. At first, I felt put on the spot having to come out of my comfort zone. Now I appreciate having the floor. Even if my comments are not reflected in the minutes, I know that I can make them a part of the minutes if I choose to do so. My research agenda is now fully supported.

Also at my current university, I am once again a program coordinator, but now I have administrative support, release time and additional compensation for the work that I do beyond the regular academic year. Additionally, as coordinator, I am now a part of a decision-making body for my department. In just one year, I became incorporated in the college (Alex-Assensoh, 2003). As a result, I feel more invested in the college and I believe that my voice is finally being heard.

As I mentioned earlier, many faculty of color complain about the disrespect that students and other faculty show them and having to prove themselves. I never experienced this but universities need to know that this happens very often to faculty of color, particularly women. Jacqueline Jordan Irvine wrote:

> Many Black academic women complain that they are victimized for simply "not looking the part" and that they are limited by racist and sexist conceptions that depict the scholar and academic as White and male. Some students and faculty assume that every Black female on campus is a member of the custodial staff. Others assume that the Black woman faculty member was hired as a result of imposed affirmative action pressures—"a two for one," satisfying the demands of Blacks and women for more representation. Some of her peers believe that she will be rewarded simply because she is Black and female. (1982, p. 114)

Knowing this, administrators can be prepared when White students come to them to complain about faculty of color. I am not suggesting that their claims be dismissed. I am suggesting that administrators inform students that if they are experiencing problems with their professor, there are protocols to be followed that should begin with the professor in question. They should also let students know that they stand behind their professors and trust their professional judgment. It has been reported that due to student complaints about a female African American professor, an administrator went into the classroom and brought in a White professor to teach the students while the professor of record watched and was told in front of students to take notes. That was reported to have taken place at my current university the year that I began.

Another contribution that I hope this research will make is for faculty of color, particularly Black female faculty who are just starting their careers in academia. In trying to make meaning of my experiences, I would caution prospective academics to research the institutions as thoroughly as possible. Find out the salary scales, course load assignments, and expectations in terms of teaching, scholarship and service. Even if you have been marginalized in other areas of your life or at other institutions, prepare yourself to speak up in terms of salary negotiations and workload assignments. Also inquire about support for research, both human and financial. Ask if mentoring is available and how professional development is supported. Arrange to talk to assistant professors of color if there are any on the faculty to gauge the support and mentoring that they are receiving or are accessible to them and how much collegiality there is. I would also suggest that diversity initiatives be investigated and know that it is likely that you will be consulted on issues of diversity or expected to assume a leadership role in diversity by virtue of your classification as a racially and/or ethnically diverse faculty member (Alex-Assensoh, 2003; Turner, 2002). Judging from my own experiences, there is comfort in being in the margins, but if change is to be made and equity is to be achieved, we must move from this place of comfort to become incorporated in the institution. Only then can change be made (Alex-Assensoh, 2003).

Due to the history of racism in our society, respect is not something that we can take for granted even at this late date in our history. In addition, we are few in number and our presence on mostly White campuses is often challenged and questioned (Irvine, 1982). Sadly, we are predisposed to the expectation of discrimination, and we are indeed the targets of discriminatory actions; however, I caution you not to assume that each behavior or statement to which you take offense is motivated by racism or sexism. Case in point: the first week at my current university, I attended a rather scholarly discussion and was the only African American present. After the meeting, a White instructor approached me and asked what I heard as "Are you 'Pat,' my new maid?"("Pat is a pseudonym that I am using here for anonymity.) At that point, I was so tired of disrespectful statements directed at African Americans that I reported the incident to the department chair who called the instructor to her office and learned that the instructor was asking if I were her new [office]mate. The resulting embarrassment could have been avoided if I had addressed the woman on the spot by asking her to repeat her question. (By the way, I confirmed that the woman was expecting a new office mate with the name that was given but I still find the terminology "new mate" instead of "new office mate" an interesting choice of words.)

Being a part of a network of other women faculty of color can be a source for encouragement and affirmation. My associations with Cynthia and other women of color in the academy have helped me tremendously in understanding and navigating the culture of White institutions, both public and private. Through these associations, my teaching and research are affirmed and supported.

Finally, as women, we have responsibilities outside of the university that men do not have ranging from child care to elder care (Tack

& Patitu, 1992). PROTECT YOUR TIME. Academia can be all-consuming; therefore, it is important to find balance between your work and your life outside of the academy. As mentioned previously, spirituality has been and continues to be my saving grace in running this race to tenure. I suggest that women faculty of color tap into their sources for inspiration and spirituality (Dillard, 2006). "'Tis grace has brought me safe thus far, and grace will lead me home…" (Newton, 1779).

References

Aguirre, A. J. (2000). *Women and minority faculty in the academic work-place: Recruitment, retention, and academic culture.* San Francisco, CA: Jossey-Bass.

Alex-Assensoh, Y. (2003). Race in the academy: Moving beyond diversity and toward the incorporation of faculty of color in predominately White colleges and universities. *Journal of Black Studies, 34*(1), 5–11.

Alfred, M.V. (2001, February). Expanding theories of career development: Adding the voices of African American women in the White academy. *Adult Education Quarterly, 51,* 108–124.

Creswell, J. W. (2007). *Qualitative inquiry and research design: Choosing among five approaches* (2nd ed.). Thousand Oaks, CA: Sage.

Dillard, C. (2006). *On spiritual strivings: Transforming an African American woman's academic life.* New York: SUNY.

Dixon-Reeves, R. (2003). Mentoring as a precursor to incorporation: An assessment of the mentoring experience of recently minted Ph.D.s. *Journal of Black Studies, 34*(1), 12–27.

hooks, b. (1990). *Yearning: Race, gender and cultural politics.* Boston: South End Press.

Irvine, J.J. (1982). The Black female academic: Doubly burdened or doubly blessed? In P. Stringer, & I. Thomas (Eds.), *Stepping off the pedestal: Academic women in the South.* (pp. 110–119) New York: Modern Language Association of America.

Ladson-Billings, G. (2000). Fighting for our lives: Preparing teachers to teach African American students. *Journal of Teacher Education, 51*(3), 206–214.

Newton, J. (1779). *Olney hymns.* London: W. Oliver.

Plata, M. (1996, Sep.). Retaining ethnic minority faculty at institutions of higher education. *Journal of Instructional Psych*ology, *23*(3), 221–

227.

Smith, W. (2008, March). Racial battle fatigue among students of color: The campus racial environment and African American males. Paper presented at Illinois State University. Normal, IL.

Tack, M., & Patitu, C.L. (1992). *Faculty job satisfaction: Women and minorities in peril.* (ASHE-ERIC Higher Education Report No. 4). Washington, DC: The George Washington University School of Education and Human Development. (ERIC Reproduction Service No. 355859).

Turner, C.S.V. (2002). Women of color in academe: Living with multiple marginality. *The Journal of Higher Education, 73*(1), 74–93.

Section Two

CHAPTER FOUR

Migrations Through Academia: Reflections of a Tenured Latina Professor

Maura I. Toro-Morn

Abstract

This essay describes and analyzes the teaching experiences—(re)(constituted here as migrations and border crossings)—of a Puerto Rican full professor at a primarily White institution in the Midwest. The experiences examined are: (1) early experiences in teaching a race relations course; and (2) teaching a Latino studies course while trying to create awareness about the need to incorporate a Latino Studies program. Through these two examples, some of the problems and challenges (as well as successes) encountered in the classroom and the pedagogic strategies which emerged as a result of these experiences are shared.

> The new mestiza copes by developing a tolerance for contradictions, a tolerance for ambiguity. She learns to be an Indian in Mexican culture, to be Mexican from an Anglo point of view. She learns to juggle cultures. She has a plural personality, she operates in a pluralistic mode—nothing is thrust out, the good, the ugly, nothing rejected, nothing abandoned. Not only does she sustain contradictions, she turns ambivalence into something else." (Anzaldua, 1987, p. 79).

Introduction

D rawing on the self-reflective traditions of feminist inquiry, I embarked on the process of writing this essay aware that in order to (re)construct my experiences as a Latina/Puerto Rican woman working in a predominantly White institution in the Midwest, a recognition of the work and struggles of the activists and intellectuals who fought to open the gates of the academy in the decades following the civil rights movements is required. It is common knowledge now that one dimension of the oppositional social movements of the 1960s and 1970s was to transform academic institutions perceived as sites of exclusion and marginalization and bastions of White, middle class, and heterosexual privilege. Feminist scholar, Chandra Mohanty (2003, p. 197) writes that "the civil rights movement, the women's movement, and other Third World liberation struggles fueled the demand for a knowledge and history of 'our own'." But more importantly, these movements sought to create paths to achieve through higher education what has been broadly constituted as the "American Dream" because historically racialized communities had been denied access to the academy as both students and faculty. Militant activism and legislation, principally in the form of Affirmative Action programs, opened predominantly White universities to unprecedented numbers of Black and Latino students and helped create academic programs to meet the needs of these neglected populations. Prestigious universities around the nation—Berkeley, Yale, and Cornel to name a few—added new courses to their curricula and created African American Studies programs (Mohanty, 2003). In 1969, the University of California at Berkeley instituted a department of ethnic studies, divided into Afro-American, Chicano, Asian-American, and Native American studies divisions (Mohanty, 2003). The development of women's studies programs was also part of this history and transformation of academia.

Feminist scholars, Frances A. Maher and Mary K. Thompson Tetreault (2007, p. 2) remind us that underrepresented groups not only "demanded entrance and full acceptance into the academy— as undergraduate and graduate students, as faculty, as scholars, and as institutional leaders" but more importantly "the new consciousness that they brought to the whole enterprise of higher education" challenged deeply held values of fairness, equality, assimilation, and what constitutes knowledge and the methods to pursue this knowledge. As Maher and Tetreault (2007, p. 2) put it "the newcomers' presence, in turn, would fuel long-term transformations in ideas about legitimate knowledge and where it comes from."

Indeed, in the past twenty years, minority scholars[1] have written an impressive number of edited books (see for example, Jacobs, Cintron, & Canton, 2002; Howell & Tuitt, 2003; Jackson & Solis-Jordan, 1999; Geok-lin Lim & Herrera-Sobek, 1999; Stanley, 2006), autobiographical books and essays (Aguirre, 2000a; Dominguez, 1994; Villanueva, 1993); and even entire journal volumes—see, for example, the *Journal of Black Studies'* September 2003 issue—devoted exclusively to describing, analyzing, and evaluating the progress and evolution of this revolution—some might say insurrection (Caban, 2003)—in academia. Added to this literature are the numerous government reports focused on the recruitment and retention of women and faculty of color (Aguirre, 2000b); Knowles & Harleston, 1997; Nieves-Squires, 1991; Tack & Patitu, 1992).

Implicit in this vast body of work are generational differences in the incorporation of racial and ethnic groups in academia. There are the "*pioneros*" and "*pioneras*" (pioneers), the celebrated leaders and organic intellectuals of the civil rights movements that called attention to how higher education was implicated in the overarching structure of racial, class, and gender oppression (Caban, 2003). These celebrated figures became part of the professoriate and helped found many academic programs, although some eventually left academia for community activism. Angela Davis, Bernice Johnson Reagon, Robert Blauner, Manning Marable, Julian Zamora, Ernesto Galarza, Frank Bonilla, Ronald Takaki, Dee Brown are a few examples of the pioneer first generation of African American, Latino, Asian, and Native American intellectuals.

Feminist scholar bell hooks (1994, p. 5) writes:

> In those days, those of us from marginal groups who were allowed to enter prestigious, predominantly White colleges were made to feel that we were there not to learn but to prove that we were the equal [to] Whites. We were there to prove this by showing how well we could become clone[s] of our peers. As we constantly confronted biases, an undercurrent of stress diminished our learning experience.

Published accounts by these *pioneros* offer painful descriptions of the virulent racism, sexism, and classism that they faced in prestigious institutions and professional associations but also affirmation that this work was shaped by, as bell hooks (1994) puts it, a "transgressive vision" and the belief in "education as the practice of freedom." Johnnella Butler (2000, p. 27) adds "most of the people of color who joined the faculties of overwhelmingly White colleges and universities over the past thirty years had hopes that their presence and work would provide possibilities and structures for an academic, cultural, social, and political change in scholarship and pedagogy."

A second generation of scholars committed to both scholarship and activism quickly followed. In the field of sociology, Becky Thompson, Patricia Hill Collins, Evelyn Nakano Glenn, Maxine Baca Zinn, and Mary Romero are prominent feminist scholars who, in my view, represent the work of second-generation scholars. Susana Chávez-Silverman (2000, p. 133) offers evidence of this generational chain when she describes how she was privileged "to study with Maria Herrera-Sobek and Alejandro Morales in one of the first national Chicano studies programs, at the University of California, Irvine." The third generation can be represented by a larger group of minorities who became part of the university expansion and growth in the aftermath of Affirmative Action policies, before these policies came under political attack and were quickly dismantled. I place myself in that third-generational group. I went to graduate school in the late 1980s and became part of academia under the auspices of the Affirmative Action policies of the 1990s.

Yet, the view emerging from new demographic data reports, second- and third-generation autobiographical accounts, and policy reports is sobering and worrisome (Garcia, 2005; Jacobs, Cintron, & Canton, 2002; Stanley, 2006). First, demographic data show entrenched racial and ethnic disparities in college enrollment, graduation, performance, and faculty recruitment. Sociologist Denise Segura (2003, p. 28) notes that at the turn of the twenty-first century "less than 1% of all full-time faculty teaching in institutions of higher education are Latina. Only 0.4 percent of full professors are Latina, 0.7 percent are associate professors, and 1.3 percent are assistant professors." By 2002, Latinos had surpassed African Americans as the largest racial and ethnic minority representing 15 percent of the total U.S. population. In 2009, the U.S. Census of Population continues to confirm the growing diversity in our communities with slightly more than one-third of the population of the United States, or 34 percent claiming a non-Anglo racial or ethnic identity and heritage. This represents an increase of 11 percent from 2000. Yet, in 2007, only 17 percent of U.S. faculty in colleges and universities are minorities (U.S. Department of Education, 2009). The prevailing metaphors in much of the new work by minority scholars suggest that we continue to be "strangers in the tower" (see, for example, Li and Beckett, 2006; Geok-lin Lim & Herrera-Sobek, 2000), "embattled scholars" (Vazquez, 1992), outsiders, "exotic others" (Dominguez, 1994), and that we are still "navigating between two worlds" (Segura, 2003). Clearly, as Mohanty (2003, p. 200) points out "decolonizing educational practices requires transformations at a number of levels, both within and outside the academy."

This chapter seeks to contribute to this growing body of autobiographical accounts by women of color who are part of the academic establishment. This is what Adalberto Aguirre (2000a) calls "academic storytelling." As Aguirre (2000a, p. 320) describes it, by assuming the role of "sociologist as narrator" of our own stories, we expose institutional practices, rules, and customs that shape our lives' as academics. The story becomes "a social event because it gives meaning to an experience nested in a complex arrangement of social relations that is known as academia" (Aguirre, 2000a, p. 320). I also use Chandra Mohanty's (2003, p. 191) meaning of the concept "personal story" not as "immediate feelings expressed confessionally" but "as something that is deeply historical and collective." She adds the meanings of the "personal (as in my story) are not static," but "they change through experience and with knowledge." This project is grounded in the notion that "one of the fundamental challenges of 'diversity' after all is to understand our collective differences in terms of historical agency and responsibility so that we can understand others and build solidarities across divisive boundaries" (Mohanty, 2003, p. 191).

The bulk of my chapter will be devoted to describing and analyzing my teaching experiences—(re)constituted here as migrations and border crossings—at a primarily White institution in the Midwest. As a full professor, I have spent nearly 20 years in the classroom. It is beyond the scope of this essay to describe all of my experiences, but I wish to draw on two specific points: (1) early experiences teaching a race relations course; (2) more recent experiences teaching a Latino studies course while trying to create awareness about the need to incorporate a Latino studies program. These examples allow me the opportunity to describe some of the problems and challenges (as well as successes) I encountered in the classroom and the pedagogic awareness born out of these engagements.

My teaching experiences are best captured by M. Jacqui Alexander's (2005) concept of "pedagogies of crossing." Each class taught and classroom entered has represented a border crossing experience for me in more ways than I can describe. The classroom has become a critical site where my multiple identities—as a Latina/Puerto Rican, immigrant/migrant, citizen/foreigner, and teacher/student—are paradoxically sites of knowledge and conflict. In the classroom, I seek to interrupt, disrupt, and transform socially constructed notions of race, ethnicity, social class, gender, and nation, among other social categories by asking students to become border crossers. My experiences in the classroom have been painful, emotionally draining, and at times intellectually devastating but also deeply transformative.

My experiences as a teacher/scholar have not been shaped by the virulent racism, sexism, or classism that the *pioneros* and those that followed them in the late 1970s faced in more and less prestigious institutions. Instead, in this paper I reflect about the particular predicaments encountered in the classroom teaching about racial, class, and gender inequality. Over the years, I have faced a range of micro-aggressions and more subtle forms of racism and sexism formulated as rhetorical strategies that Eduardo Bonilla-Silva (2006) calls the new tropes of color-blind racism characteristic of the post-civil rights era.[2] These strategies are deployed in the classroom by students who come from fairly homogeneous communities and who do not want to be troubled by a view of the world that disrupts their sense of belonging and privilege.[3] This view of the world is also supported by an institutional culture, values, and practices that continue to perceive minority

students and faculty of color as groups that need to be added as the
formula to create diversity across campus. In that context, this chapter
seeks to deconstruct the institutional ideological bedrock of assumptions that continues to delay and impede the goal of achieving and
institutionalizing diversity as a core goal and value. I argue that institutionally the "additive model" continues to be the dominant paradigm to addressing minority issues in educational institutions that
did not face the kind of turmoil engendered by oppositional struggle
of the 1960s and 1970s. The cumulative stock of these experiences af-
firms to me that:

> ...the academy and the classroom itself are not mere sites of instructions.
> They are also political and cultural sites that represent accommodations and
> contestations over knowledge by differently empowered social constituen-
> cies. The teachers and students produce, reinforce, recreate, resist, and trans-
> form ideas about race, gender, and difference in the classroom. Also, the
> academic institutions in which we are located create similar paradigms,
> canons, and voices that embody and transcribe race and gender"(Mohanty,
> 2003, p. 194).

This chapter will be organized in the following fashion: In the
next section, I describe the methodological strategies I have used to
reconstruct the experiences I present here. A brief account of the
unique institutional history of Illinois State University and its efforts
at attracting minority faculty follows. In keeping with the title of this
chapter, I describe how migration and border crossing have shaped
my teaching and scholarly work. I began my educational journey as a
political science major in a small liberal arts college, Interamerican
University, on the West coast of Puerto Rico. I migrated from Puerto
Rico to the U.S. to pursue graduate studies in 1983. From 1983–1993, I
pursued graduate studies at Illinois State University, University of
Connecticut, and Loyola University. Most of my academic career has
been devoted to studying migrations, people in movement, crossing

borders real and imagined. I, too, have crossed many borders in an attempt to find an intellectual home in sociology, ethnic studies, feminist studies and, now more recently, Latino Studies. Each space has been complicated for me for different reasons. I will describe how this border crossing experience has shaped my development as a scholar and my vision of the future of the academy. Today my life, like my academic work, exists in a transnational space. The last section of the chapter is then devoted to my teaching experiences in two classroom settings. This ambitious narrative is historical, introspective, personal, and I hope deeply sociological in that I attempt to raise larger issues facing faculty of color in educational institutions across the nation.

The Ethnographic Research Tradition: A Word about Methods

As a sociologist, I have been deeply influenced by the ethnographic research tradition. Trained in Chicago (Loyola University of Chicago) by scholars educated in the Chicago-style ethnographic tradition, I continue to embrace key principles of this research method while recognizing new efforts to describe and analyze social phenomena, such as autoethnography (Ellis, 2004). I use a triangulation of methods—institutional ethnography, autoethnography, and participant observations—to develop a narrative that describes selected moments of my experiences as a teacher-scholar working in a predominantly White institution in the Midwest. Methodologically, this chapter is ambitious in that I attempt to offer a narrative that accounts for the unique institutional history of Illinois State University and its efforts at attracting minority scholars (institutional ethnography), my own history and experiences as the first Latina/Puerto Rican scholar hired in the department of Sociology and Anthropology (autoethnography), and evolving insights generated as a participant observer. Feminist theory and research methods principles have also shaped my work as a scholar and the work I present here.

The autoethnographic method represents a recent development in the ethnographic research tradition. Some call it an "emerging art" (Duncan, 2004), while others view it as "an intriguing and promising qualitative method that offers a way of giving voice to personal experience for the purpose of extending sociological understanding" (Wall, 2008, p. 38). Sarah Wall (2008) writes that "autoethnographers vary in their emphasis on auto-(self), -ethno-(the sociocultural connection), and graphy (the application of the research process)." Others have defined autoethnography as a systematic sociological introspection. A consensus is beginning to emerge that this new method, although untested and at times controversial, shares some key principles of doing an autoethnography.

In the interest of self-disclosure, I did not set out to write an autoethnography. I have, however, come to recognize that much of what I am doing here can be considered part of this new and evolving method. I have searched my personal diaries, teaching portfolio, lecture notes, syllabi, student evaluations, and other teaching notes for evidence of the evolution, struggles, resolutions, and problems I have faced working at a predominantly White institution. Collectively, this evidence offers the most theoretical insight to the goals of this volume. I have used key institutional publications and documents to offer a brief historical account of the institution and its efforts to recruit minority faculty. I have also relied on observations generated over the years that I have spent in the institution as a faculty member. In revisiting institutional documents, I realized that I had accumulated a perspective on the institutional history that I offer in this essay as a participant observer. I defined myself as a reflective practitioner. In other words, I have spent a great deal of my career reflecting on my pedagogy, the classroom, my relationships with students, and my sense of self and evolution as a scholar/teacher. Thus, this autoethnography has been twenty years in the making.

The Institutional Setting: Illinois State University

It is common knowledge that the university system in the United States is highly stratified, bifurcated, and undergoing a profound transformation under the auspices of current globalization and privatization strategies (Maher and Tetreault, 2007; Mohanty, 2003). One manifestation of this bifurcation can be represented in the division of universities into comprehensive research universities and predominantly teaching institutions. The stratification of universities is more complex in that there are private and public Ivys, flagship state universities, third-tier and fourth-tier universities, a vast array of community colleges, and the emerging web-based universities. Universities are also stratified by disciplines and departments. State disinvestment as a major source of funding for public institutions and the increasing competition for resources have intensified and sharpened the hierarchy of academic institutions around the nation. Historian John Freed (2009) argues that "part of the paradox of Illinois State's position in the educational hierarchy" lies in the fact that "while it repeatedly asserted its commitment to affordability and diversity, its location in Central Illinois, tuition increases as state funding declined, and laudable efforts to raise admission and academic standards have had the opposite effect."

Illinois State University's (ISU) history lies in the peculiar niche of "normal schools," colleges founded to train teachers for the growing number of public schools that needed qualified instructors. The college was established in 1857 as a teachers college and although this is a source of institutional prestige and pride, it has also been the source of some institutional confusion. It is beyond the scope of this chapter to offer a full account of the institution's history, but it is important to point out some critical points in the institutional development of ISU.

Illinois State defines itself as "Illinois' first public university," "an institution of first choice for increasing numbers of academically talented and motivated students" (Illinois State University, 2008b). It claims to "have a strong commitment to scholarship and to undergraduate and graduate education" (Illinois State University, 2008b). The stated core values of the institution are pursuit of learning and scholarship, individualized attention, public opportunity, civic engagement, and diversity. Diversity has been defined as "informed respect for differences among students, faculty, and staff by fostering an inclusive environment characterized by ethical behavior and social justice that prepares students to be fully engaged participants in a global society. The University endeavors to create a varied and inclusive community where all students are active participants in a global society characterized by teamwork, respect for differences, civic engagement, and educational goals which celebrate diversity" (Illinois State University, 2008a).

Juxtaposed to the stated vision of the university is the reality of the socio-demographics of the institution, which raises many questions about the viability of such vision. The lived experiences of its minority students and faculty of color suggest that there is still a lot more work to be done to fully achieve the goal of diversity both demographically and institutionally. In 1993, the year I joined the faculty of the sociology program, there were 703 tenured/tenure track (106 non-tenure) faculty members in the university, of these 4.6 (N = 32) percent were Asian-Pacific Islanders, 3.0 (N = 21) percent African Americans, and 1 percent (N = 8) Hispanics. Five were in the College of Arts and Sciences. According to ISU's fact book, there were no Latinos in the Colleges of Education and Fine Arts. In 2008, the faculty ranks continued to be predominantly White (87 percent), and the faculty of color continued to be embarrassingly few: Hispanics/Latinos represented 2.1 (N = 25) percent of the tenured/tenure track faculty; 3.0 were African Americans, and 5.0 were Asian-Pacific Islanders.

The underrepresentation of minorities in the faculty ranks at ISU and statewide has prompted a series of reports and investigations by the Illinois Board of Higher Education (IBHE). The IBHE (2003, p. 7) observes that most students have "at best only occasional contact with African American and Latino faculty." In Illinois, African American and Latino faculty tend to be over-concentrated in Chicago, with ten institutions employing 53 percent of all African American faculty and 42 percent of all Latino faculty. This means that "nearly two hundred thousand students enrolled at the other 50 public institutions in Illinois have less than two in fifty chance of being taught by an African American faculty member and less than one in fifty chance of being taught by a Latino faculty member" (IBHE, 2003, p. 7). The abysmally low numbers of African American and Latino faculty is a serious problem because "it will take more than one hundred years at current growth rates" for both groups to "reach the level of representation in faculty ranks that they now have in the state's population (that is 14.9 percent for African Americans and 12.3 percent for Latinos)" (IBHE, 2003, p. 8).

Anthropologist Virginia Dominguez (1994) writes that "diversity talk" is currently at a premium in universities across the nation. "Diversity" has become a code word invoked in strategic planning, hiring documents, curricular offerings, and vision statements. The tendency is to invoke a surface-level interest, a "celebration" in all forms of diversity devoid of deeper meaning. The "referent is always specific excluded, marginalized, or underempowered groups typically within the United States" (Dominguez, 1994, p. 334), but without any acknowledgment of the particular historical location of the groups subject to exclusion and marginalization. The problem is that a particular construction of difference and otherness becomes objectified, commodified, and (re)constructed in "deeply racialized ways"

(Dominguez, 1994, p. 334). In other words, "racialization takes place when differences between human beings are simplified and transformed into Difference, overvaluing particular bodily differences by imbuing them with lasting meaning." Talk of "diversity" fosters what Chandra Mohanty (2003, p. 200) calls "empty cultural pluralism." Mohanty (1993) draws on the work of Henry Giroux and his "pedagogy of normative pluralism" to describe this notion of how we come to "occupy separate, different, and equally valuable places" as individuals representing specific groups. This form of cultural pluralism, diversity, or multiculturalism dehistoricizes the experiences of minority groups and "makes possible the management of race in the name of cooperation and harmony" (Mohanty, 2003, p. 204). Implicit in these ideological constructions lies the deeply problematic "additive model to diversity," that is the notion that simply adding people of color (be that students and faculty) we achieve diversity without upsetting the foundation of the institution.

This is the institutional context that promotes what Alyssa Garcia (2005, p. 261) has labeled the "commodification of race and gender" and "cultural taxation" processes encountered by faculty of color across academia. More broadly, faculty of color are recruited to address problems of absence, underrepresentation, and/or—though frequently not overtly stated—as tokens. There is a vast volume of studies showing that once recruited frequently faculty of color find themselves isolated, ghettoized, and overburdened with committee and service assignments (Garcia, 2005; Segura, 2003). A dimension of the commodification of race and gender presents itself in different aspects of faculty service. Drawing on the work of William Tierney, Garcia (2005, p. 266) states that "faculty of color do four times the amount of service as that of their White colleagues." Adalberto Aguirre (2000a, p. 320) writes, "during my tenure as a faculty member in academia, I have served in numerous committees, especially the affirmative action committee, and participated in activities that have focused on faculty recruitment." Mohanty (2003, p. 212) adds "our voices are carefully placed and domesticated: one in history, one in English, perhaps one in the sociology department." For those of us who somehow have managed to "survive in the academy" (Vazquez, 1992), we find ourselves complicitous in the construction of this commodified diversity. We allow university photographers to take pictures of us with students for university brochures and other publications, and we allow ourselves one more committee assignment, recruitment committee (service commitments that at the time of tenure and promotion evaluation count for very little) with the deeply held belief that it is our ethical, political, and professional responsibility. Again, Jessi Vasquez (1992, p. 1045) describes the dilemmas of minority faculty in predominantly White institutions:

> as a committed faculty member, you take on more and more, because you believe that there is no other choice…You move into a new area, or you take on the added burden of yet another committee, only because you know — or think you know — that the job will not get done….you may be one of two or three Puerto Ricans, if that many on campus, who is in the right department and division, and so you feel obliged, nay compelled — politically, socially, pedagogically — to join the effort, because you sense that the presence of that project or service on campus will make a difference in the university and ultimately in the community.

The end result of these experiences is feeling exhausted, overworked, overextended frequently at the expense of your research/scholarly agenda and family responsibilities. To add insult to injury, when we do raise the issues of the lack of diversity or the need for diversity in a new administrative hire we are frequently dismissed as "having an agenda" (Alicea, 1999) or "acting on narrow self-interest" (Garcia, 2005). Indeed, a vacuous diversity ideology promoted at the expense of the work of minority faculty continues to make the university a "chilly" environment for faculty of color, and ISU is no exception.

Notes Toward an Autobiography: Migrations and Crossing Borders

> You are a child of the Américas,
> a light skinned mestiza of the Caribbean,
> a child of many diaspora, born into this continent at a crossroads…
>
> I am Caribeña, island grown. Spanish is in my flesh,
> ripples from my tongue, lodges in my hips…
> I am of Latinoamerica, rooted in the history of my continent:
> I speak from that body. (Morales and Morales, 1986, p. 447)

As a light-skinned "child of the Américas," my life has been shaped by the processes of migration and the experience of crossing borders (both real and imagined). Both my mother and father's family represent significant chapters of the labor migration movement that took Puerto Ricans to the United States, mostly to New York.[4] In fact, the idea to empirically study the experiences of Puerto Rican women in the migration process developed from a conversation I had with my *Abuela* (Mama Isabel, paternal grandmother) during one of my frequent visits to the Island during graduate school. Intrigued by our conversation, I turned to the growing body of published literature about Puerto Rican migration only to find out that women's experiences in the migration process were absent from the literature and when present they were frequently depicted as followers of men, with very little agency of their own. As a consequence, I have spent a significant part of my academic and scholarly career documenting their migration experiences (Toro-Morn, 1995, 1999); work experiences (Toro-Morn, 1999); as agents in the formation of U.S. communities (Toro-Morn, 2005); dealing with family issues (Toro-Morn, 2004); and the gendered experiences of second- and third-generation children of immigrants (Toro-Morn & Alicea, 2003).

I added a chapter to the family's history of migration when the opportunity to pursue graduate studies in the Midwest presented itself. My migration, however, was part of what I have come to identify as part of the "Puerto Rican brain drain," the movement of educated Puerto Ricans to continue our education in U.S. universities (Toro-Morn, 1995, 2005). Educated and professional Puerto Ricans have become incorporated as part of the immigrant professional social classes (teachers, engineers, accountants, among others) in the United States. The "brain drain" extends to other segments of the Latino community. The migration of educated and professional Puerto Ricans became more pronounced in the 1980s and 1990s (Aranda, 2007). According to anthropologist Jorge Duany (in press), the migration of elite Puerto Ricans has intensified in the last five years, and it has shifted to a new site of settlement, Orlando, Florida. The movement of working class and educated Puerto Ricans and their incorporation in the U.S. labor market has been rooted in the twin forces of colonialism and globalization, processes that have also shaped the educational experiences of Puerto Ricans both here and abroad.

As a Latina intellectual, migrations and border crossing have also shaped my academic career. As a Puerto Rican woman, I have struggled to find an intellectual home in sociology, ethnic studies, feminist studies and now more recently Latino Studies. Each space has been complicated for me for different reasons. Sociology was a complicated space for me because I selected to study topics that at the time did not seem mainstream (gender, migration, intersectionality), and I sought to deploy principles and assumptions drawn from my engagement with feminist theory and methods. I became adept at crossing intellectual borders, at speaking different languages, and recognizing potential dangers.

My experience in the academy represents one dimension of the rather recent, yet significant, incorporation of Latina/o intellectuals into American universities. The ethno-cultural landscape of this incorporation follows very closely the migration and formation of Latina/o communities across the nation and can be traced to the civil rights movement of the 1960s and 1970s. In the West and Southwest, the Chicano/a movement sought to call attention to the experiences of second- and third-generation children of Mexican immigrants. In California, through vigorous demonstrations, strikes, and sit-ins, Chicanos fought for the creation of academic programs connected to community empowerment (Caban, 2003). On the East Coast, Blacks and Puerto Ricans "took over the walled-in South Campus of the City College of New York and closed the university until the board of trustees agreed to establish a School of Black and Puerto Rican Studies" (Caban, 2003, p. 11). According to Caban (2003, p. 12) "Chicano and Puerto Rican studies disavowed the assimilationist discourse and eschewed social science positivism as a static and ahistorical mode of analysis ill suited to the task of reclaiming a history long denied." In the late 1970s and 1980s, a number of academic programs and research centers were born out of this activism, followed by the establishment of professional associations helping to establish legitimate intellectual communities. The creation and institutionalization of key journals such as *Atzlan*, *The Centro Journal*, and in the Midwest, the *Latino Studies Journal* (later to become Latino Studies), reinscribed the history of this ethno-cultural landscape as the key publication outlets for the field.

I entered this ethno-intellectual landscape as a graduate student in the Midwest in the late 1980s, a location with a history that has yet to be written. When I became a graduate student at Illinois State University in 1983, the institution did not offer any graduate programs to study Black and Latino issues. There was an incipient women's studies program, but its offerings were limited to a handful of courses peppered in the social sciences. There was an undergraduate minor in Latin American, Caribbean, and Latino studies organized by a historian, but it had very little institutional support and visibility.

When I returned to ISU as a faculty member in the early 1990s, there had been very little progress in terms of the development of programs and academic offerings focused on Black and Latino issues at both the undergraduate and graduate levels. It was in 2002, under the auspices of Professor Roberta Trites, interim dean of the College of Arts and Sciences, that a group of faculty was organized to discuss the formal establishment of a Latino studies program. It is beyond the scope of this chapter to trace the rather complex history of the program that we have today. In the fall, 2007 an internal search was conducted in the College of Arts and Sciences and I was offered the position of Director of Latin American and Latina/o Studies Program. We reside, though not officially, in the College of Arts and Sciences. The program offers undergraduate students a minor but no graduate concentration. We do not have an office on campus, a space we can call our own. Our budget consists of contributions from other colleges in the university and we do not have official personnel. I accepted this position out of my political and pedagogical belief that it is time for ISU to have such a program, a conviction born of my own experiences as a Latina/Puerto Rican woman in academia.

Pedagogies of Crossing: Overview of Classroom Experiences

In this section, I turn to analyzing my experiences in the classroom, in particular teaching two courses that have come to represent different border crossings for me: (1) Sociology 264, Minority Relations, an elective in the sociology program; and (2) Sociology 109, Introduction to the U.S. Latina/o Experience, a fairly new course in the program and the university, implemented as part of the revisions in the general education program. These two courses represent different dimensions of the frustrations, difficulties, and struggles found in the classroom.

I was hired to address curricular needs in the field of race and ethnic relations stemming from the departure of the previous hire who had been denied tenure. When I joined the sociology program, Sociology 264, Minority Relations, was a course required for social work majors and was an elective course for other programs as well; thus, there was (and still is) a need in the department to teach multiple sections of this course. A typical teaching load for me was two sections of Sociology 264 (about 45–50 students in each class) and one other core course (senior experience) or graduate course. In the pages that follow, I describe some of the dimensions of that frustration and the paradox that underlies my role in the classroom.

As a "child of the Americas," a *Mestiza consciousness* represents my epistemic point of departure to teaching about inequality. In other words, as a Latina/Puerto Rican woman, immigrant, Spanish-speaking, daughter of a factory worker in an export-processing zone, I developed a course that required students to move away from the dichotomous ways of thinking about race, thus beginning to recognize the multiplicity of sources of inequality and differentiation in the American experience. In fact, the first day of classes was spent addressing the disclaimer that this class was not "a make me feel good about America" course but a critical engagement with our history, the legacy of exploitation and subordination, and our future. In the syllabus I proposed to offer an opportunity to reflect about inequality in American society. I wrote: "this class will offer you the opportunity to read and reflect upon the social constructions of race/ethnicity, class, gender, and sexual identity and how these categories are transformed into systems of inequality both in the U.S. and globally. Race/ethnicity, class, and gender are important dimensions in our lives, they shape our sense of self-worth, the types of jobs we get, where we live, and how much power we have. Consequently, this class is designed to understand how race, class, and gender dynamics have shaped ourselves, our communities, and society in general." Underlying this description is the intersectionality framework that has been so important in the development of my scholarly work. I devoted a significant part of my early teaching career to unpacking and deconstructing the black/white paradigm underlying the social construction of race.

Teaching Race and Ethnic Relations in the Heartland

I begin this section with a poignant diary entry from 2001, the summer I returned to teaching after a year sabbatical, my first since tenure. Summer classes can be very intense because you are in class Monday–Thursday for three hours, yet it is clear in the following quote that I had found myself in more than familiar territory.

Uno nunca sabe lo que tiene hasta que lo pierde!!! (You never know how good you have it until it is gone.) That's how I would summarize my first week of classes after my sabbatical. Quite a rough week in so many ways! It is 5:36 in the morning, and I cannot sleep so I must write my thoughts down in an attempt to process both intellectually and emotionally what is happening to me. I need to do it in order to be able to return to the classroom and move myself into a different space....Returning to teaching has been so hard and disruptive that it has made me physically ill. I woke up with a horrendous sore neck that sent me running to the masseuse. While resting on the masseuse's table quietly, it came to me: this class has taken (and continues to take) a toll on me because as a teacher and a person of color I am asked to do two things that seem contradictory.

I have to teach students about racial and ethnic inequality and become the recipient of their own defensiveness and resistance to recognizing inequality in American society. On the other hand, as they go through the process of learning, resistance, learning, I become the repository of all of their negative cultural baggage about inequality. Although such struggle is an important process in the steps of learning, they are dumping their stuff on me. As a woman of color, it is so hard…I too become defensive and resentful that I have to do that for them.

As a woman of color, the classroom is not a safe space for me to talk about these issues. The contradictory role of teacher and person of color teaching about race and ethnic inequality places me in two hierarchies at once; student/teacher hierarchy; White and person of color hierarchy.

All of these things, then, become all the more difficult because I don't teach other classes that offer me a rest from such tangled hierarchies. On top of that, teaching at a predominantly White university further complicates this because I feel so alone. Although some of my colleagues experience the struggles of teaching and student resistance to learning, they don't experience it from the perspective of being a person of color teaching about issues of inequality. Students also learn to think of minorities as "ghetto instructors." That is students only encounter minority instructors in classes that deal with "minority" issues; thus, they too learn by association that minority issues are only dealt with by minority instructors.

I am tired of that and I want out…out of here. I enjoy teaching this class because it is something that interests me intellectually and personally, but I must let it go if I want to keep my mental health and sanity. I want to teach classes that deal with the Latino situation. I want to leave, move to another university, find a place with more Latinos….

There are three points in my diary narrative that deserve elaboration and analysis. First, there is evidence of the physical and emotional toll that teaching and working in the academy has had (and continues to have) on me. This is an issue that has been addressed by the growing body of personal, biographical and autobiographical essays written by people of color in the academy (see, for example, Garcia, 2005; Jacobs, Cintron, & Canton, 2002; Jackson & Jordan, 1999).

The paradoxical position that I have come to occupy in the class-room deserves elaboration here. As a woman of color, I am teaching a class that exposes students, in particular White students, to the issue of White privilege, an issue that many of them are intellectually and emotionally unprepared to handle. Fortunately, over the last ten years there has been an explosion of scholarly work about whiteness; thus, I have had within my reach thoughtful and provocative essays written by well-known scholars such as Allan Johnson, Peggy McIntosh, Ruth Frankenberg, and ISU's Alison Bailey and Tom Gershick. Students perceived my lectures about White privilege as "she hates White people," a statement that I frequently found in my student evaluations. Alongside the denial of White privilege, there were other familiar tropes: "my family didn't own any slaves, what do you mean by social collective responsibility"; "slavery is over, can we stop talking about it?"; and the ubiquitous "aren't we all human beings after all?" Ironically, one of the ways that I moved students, predominantly White students from a place of resistance to unlearning racism was by asking them to write about their own experiences as raced, classed, and gendered individuals. Readings in the class offered students the opportunity to read autobiographical accounts of others who had struggled with those issues, thus offering role models of autobiographical writing.

In applying some elements of feminist pedagogy I am aware that I was "no angel in the classroom," to borrow Bernice Malka Fisher's (2001) phrase. I encouraged student reflection, openness to voicing their views (even when they were expressly racist, sexist, or classist), because I hoped to foster also an awareness of social justice. At the end of that summer class, I started thinking about creating a course dealing with the Latino experience, a topic I discuss next.

Looking for *Terra Firma*:
Teaching Introduction to U.S. Latina/o Studies

The opportunity to create a course dealing with the Latino experience presented itself when the university underwent a revamping of the general education program.[5] Having achieved promotion and tenure, I felt a degree of freedom to create a course that was closer to my research areas of interest and that did not deplete my intellectual and emotional energy. I designed and developed Sociology 109, Introduction to U.S. Latina/o Studies, a course in the U.S. Traditions section that students take for general education credit. The newly developed general education program was formed under the auspices of what has come to be known institutionally as Educating Illinois. Educating Illinois describes the mission of ISU as to provide "a broad, common foundation of study upon which to build an undergraduate education" (Illinois State University, 2008a). The program has four major goals: (1) critical inquiry and problem solving; (2) public opportunity; (3) diverse and global perspectives; (4) life-long learning. "Diverse and global perspectives" indicates that "students will be exposed to diverse and global perspectives by developing and communicating an appreciation for the impact made in personal and professional lives" (Illinois State University, 2008a).

Through the process of curricular review and evaluation, I argued that the development of the course coincided with the demographic shift that took place in the country as Latinos surpassed African Americans as the largest racial/ethnic minority in the United States and represented an attempt to address, in a serious way, the lack of knowledge about Latinos in our curriculum, a gap that continues today since few course offerings address Latino issues. Introduction to Latina/o Studies has become a popular course in the university and an important avenue for students wishing to pursue a minor in Latin American and Latino Studies.

I define my approach to teaching Introduction to U.S. Latina/o Studies (Sociology 109), as transnational. That is, the course does not only study Latinos as an emerging new racial group in the United States and their process of adaptation and assimilation, but it also offers a distinct transnational (trans-global) perspective by addressing in a significant part of the course the differences in the colonial heritages of Spanish and Anglo-Saxon colonization, U.S./Latin American foreign relations, and most recent events connected to North American Free Trade Agreement (NAFTA) and Central American Free Trade Agreement (CAFTA). In other words, my approach to teaching Latino Studies is an important lesson about our current global moment, namely, that the creation and enforcement of artificial boundaries (insiders/outsiders), the intellectual separation of communities (here/there) does not allow us to fully understand the complexity of the Latino experience, a group that is clearly different from European immigrant groups that arrived earlier in U.S. history.

Very quickly I learned that Latino Studies could not provide me the *terra firma* I had been searching for in the classroom. Very quickly similar issues had surfaced in Sociology 264 and magnified themselves in a number of ways. Student perceptions of the class available in "Rate My Professor" web site indicates how some students perceive the class and my teaching. One student wrote: "this class was awful. The teacher was very biased and only wanted you to learn what she had to say." Another student wrote "very interesting course, will open your mind to some new concepts and broaden your horizons." Following is a graduate student's observation of a confrontation that took place in the classroom when I apparently lost my cool.

> I think the students were exposed to a lot of new things yesterday and it was
> an important learning experience for students who are not exposed to much
> diversity. The truth cannot be sugarcoated and some reactions only served

to highlight the structural racism present inside the class. I don't think many students have been exposed to the Latino experience other than what they have learned from their families or in school. Throughout the semester, I have observed two reactions in the class. One reaction to any discussion of racism is tantamount to a hatred of White people and refusal to participate. Another reaction victimizes the Latino experience, attempting to prove they themselves hold no prejudices, their continued participation however, ultimately exposes the prejudice they refuse to address. Neither of these reactions leads to a better understanding of the Latino experience because neither examines White privilege, one of the most influential foundations of the Latino historical, political and social history and present. The people of color in class (all 5 of us), understood what you were talking about. I don't think you were wrong; I think we have been skirting around this issue all semester and I'm glad you brought it up. All semester we have talked about one part of the Latino experience, the history, 'assimilation,' citizenship, music, television. *West Side Story* and the subsequent discussion highlighted the other part of the Latino experience: being paranoid, the double standard, getting angry, being invalidated and rejected by those who chose to be ignorant of a privilege they alone enjoy. I think our talk yesterday put up a mirror to each of these students and asked them to take a look at themselves and the privileges they enjoy at other's expense. I find few professors willing to do this, and I commend you for challenging them more than they have ever been asked to do. And in accordance with our experience, you always have to ask yourself: how would they have reacted if you were a White man and said these things? I think student reactions to the topic and the discussion exemplify the endemicity of a subconscious White privilege. I think you know I'm one of the more radical people in that class, maybe I'm the wrong person to ask because I support addressing these issues with respect and passion.

At another level, teaching Sociology 109 is deeply rewarding because of the number of Latino students who find themselves in my class. Here is a note from a student that is particularly revealing. On one level, it highlights the prejudice and racism that Latino students encounter from other students; it shows evidence of how students continue to perceive the work of professors who, like myself, challenge them to see the world from a different perspectives; but more importantly it offers evidence of the transformative process of learning.

> I can't even begin to tell you how differently your class made me look at the world around me, not just as a strong Latina, which now I am proud to call myself, but simply as a human being who expected the people around me to be more socially aware and sensitive.
>
> The night after the final, I went home and I cried. Not because the final was stressful or even anything to do with the material that was covered, but because of the day that I had that led up to that final. I spent the hours leading up to the final studying with a study group that consisted of 3 other students in the class who I was friends with prior to taking this class. I had already been aware of their wary views of the material we studied in class, but I had no idea how their insensitivity and objection to broadening their awareness would become evident during these few hours.
>
> They unleashed their hurtful and often prejudiced comments, even though they were aware of my racial background, and it dawned on me the reason they weren't afraid of making these comments in front of me because they saw my complexion, my diction and my personality to be close enough to theirs, close enough to being "White" that they didn't see how much their words hurt me.
>
> But it wasn't their words that still stuck with me, even 6 hours after I heard them, that made me cry later that night. What made me cry was the fact that not once had, I opened my mouth to defend not only myself but my ancestors who made the life possible that I live today.
>
> I've sat with their words and my regrets for a week now and have decided that I will not let myself be silenced any longer. With your help, Professor Toro-Morn, I know that minoring in Latino/a Studies is the first step I can take to de-silence not only myself, but millions of others. I am aware that a minor in Latino studies might not be the most practical minor to go along with a major in speech pathology, but I decided that life is not always about practicality. I don't want to look back on my life and see that it was void of passion for the topics I feel so strongly about, no matter how diverse those topics may be.

Thank you for changing my perspective on the world this past few months. It is one of the greatest gifts anyone could have given me.

Lupe Santos[6]

Lupe's account, though painful, is important because it awakened in her the desire to learn more about herself and her heritage, it also exposed her to the deeply felt prejudices that exist toward Latinos, thus making the need to continue this class all the more imperative.

Looking Back, Looking Forward: Quixotic Endeavors

Christine Stanley (2006) writes that the experiences of faculty of color at predominantly White institutions have been private for far too long. She adds "if we do not acknowledge these experiences as legitimate or if we continue to espouse the rhetoric of having a diverse academic community that is representative of the talent in our nation without learning from the experiences of the people we work to recruit and retain" then little will change in academic institutions across the nation. The experiences I have offered in this chapter, though deeply personal, are offered with the hope of creating such change. The experiences I have offered here represent the accumulated knowledge, insight, and reflection of over twenty years of crossing borders in the heartland of America. The journey has not been easy, the accumulated experiences at times difficult and painful to understand, but I continue to do it again, and again, and again, persuaded by the idea that education is "the practice of freedom" (hooks, 1994). Drawing on the work of Jacqui M. Alexander (2005, p. 8) a pedagogy of crossing is also "meant to evoke/invoke the crossroads, the space of convergence and endless possibility; the place where we put down and discard the unnecessary in order to pick up what is necessary. It is that imaginary from which we dream the craft of a new compass."

Notes

I want to dedicate this chapter to the following graduate students, the next generation of scholars in the process of becoming part of academia: Andrea Silva (Politics and Government), Jose Castellanos and Meghan Sparling (English), Maria Luisa Zamudio (Education), Dan Kappus and Makoto Sakamoto (Sociology). Our journeys crossed at Illinois State University.

1 A word about language seems relevant here. There is no single word that can do justice to the multiplicity of social locations and identities that we embody as individuals and as members of community groups. I am aware of the conceptual problems with the concept of minority group (see Meyers (1984) for a detailed description of its history and legacy) and other pan-ethnic labels such as Asian American, Latino/Hispanic, and Native American. I also recognize that the labels used in this paper are socially constructed categories and legacies of specific historical periods. My awareness has been influenced by the groundbreaking work of Winant (2000) and Eduardo Bonilla-Silva (2006).

2 It is important to point out that the classroom is not the only site where I have experienced these micro-aggressions. I have also experienced these issues in the university and the local community.

3 Yet another caveat: Not all White students were the source of these tensions. To be sure, there were some White males and a greater number of White female students, some of them sociology and women's studies minors, who became allies in the classroom. These students were able to challenge their classmates on their implicit racism, something I could not do as a woman of color. Some White students had learned to cross borders as part of their formative high school experiences and thus entered the classroom with some intuitive knowledge of what was happening. There were a lot of exchanges between White students and minority students that were heated, contentious, and emotionally difficult. Although I frequently intervened, there had been many times in which emotions ran deep and were not resolved, a characteristic of the race terrain in this country.

4 My father's mother's, Mama Isabel, had lived and worked in New York in the 1940s and 1950s during the most significant movement of Puerto Ricans to New York City. The same day I learned that many of my aunts and uncles were also part of this movement. While many of father's relatives eventually returned to the Island, my mother's family history of migration is much more complicated. Her

brother and young wife left the Island seeking a better life for themselves. Eventually, they divorced, and my uncle, breaking with traditional gender expectations, won custody of the three children. As a single father, he needed help caring for his children and that is how my mother found herself an immigrant in New York City.

5 I had already participated in the creation of a class, American Diversity, for the newly revamped general education program. This class addressed the rather tumultuous history of race relations in the country with the hopes that it offered students an opportunity to create alternative accounts of American history. The creation of that class represents an example of the political collaboration with like-minded colleagues, such as Tom Gershick, who shared a vision of diversity that is deeply transformative.

6 The name of the student is a pseudonym in order to protect her identity. For the record, I asked student's permission to use her electronic note here.

References

Aguirre, A. (2000a). Academic storytelling: A critical race theory of affirmative action. *Sociological Perspectives, 43*(2), 319–339.

Aguirre, A. J. (2000b). Women and minority faculty in the academic workplace: Recruitment, retention, and academic culture. *ASHE-ERIC Higher Education Report*, Vol. 27, No. 6. San Francisco, CA: Jossey-Bass.

Alexander, J. M. (2005). *Pedagogies of crossing: Meditations on feminism, sexual politics, memory and the sacred*. Durham: Duke University Press.

Alicea. M. (1999). Acaso No Soy Maestra Tambien? (Ain't I a teacher too?). In S. Jackson & and J. Solis Jordan (Eds.), *I've got a story to tell: Identity and place in the academy* (pp.35–43). New York: Peter Lang.

Anzaldua. G. (1987). *Borderlands, la frontera: The new Mestiza.* San Francisco: Aunt Lute Books.

Aranda, E. (2007). *Emotional bridges to Puerto Rico: Migration, return migration, and the struggles of incorporation.* Lanham, MD: Rowman and Littlefield.

Bonilla-Silva, E. (2006). *Racism without racism: Color-blind racism and the persistence of racial inequality in the United States.* Lanham, MD: Rowman and Littlefield.

Butler, J. E. (2000). Reflections on borderlands and the Color Line. In S. G. Lim & M. Herrera-Sobek (Eds.), *Power, race, and gender in the academe: Strangers in the tower?* (pp. 8–31). New York: The Modern Language Association of America.

Caban, P. (2003). Moving from the margins to where? Three decades of Latino/a studies. *Latino Studies, 1*, 5–53.

Chàvez-Silverman. S. (2000). Tropicalizing the liberal arts college classroom. In S. Geok-lin Lim & Herrera-Sobek, M. (Eds.), *Power, race and gender in the academy: Strangers in the tower?* (pp. 132–153). New York: The Modern Language Association of America.

Dominguez, V. (1994). A taste for 'the other': Intellectual complicity in racializing practices. *Current Anthropology, 35*(4): 333–348.

Duany, J. (in press). The Orlando-Ricans: Overlapping identity discourses among elite Puerto Rican immigrants. *Centro: Journal of the Center for Puerto Rican Studies.*

Duncan, M. (2004). Autoethongraphy: Critical appreciation of an emerging art. *International Journal of Qualitative Methods, 3*(4), Article 3. Retrieved June 6, 2009, from http://www.ualberta.ca/~iiqm/backissues/3_4/html/duncan.html.

Ellis, C. (2004). *The ethnographic I: A methodological novel about autoethnography.* Walnut Creek, CA: AltaMira Press.

Fisher, B.M. (2001). *No angel in the classroom: Teaching through feminist discourse.* Lanham, MD: Rowman and Littlefield.

Freed, J.B. (2009). *Educating Illinois: Illinois State University, 1857–2007.* Normal: Illinois State University.

Garcia, A. (2005). Counter stories of race and gender: Situating experiences of Latinas in the academy. *Latino Studies, 3,* 261–273.

Geok-lin Lim, S. & Herrera-Sobek, M. (2000). *Power, race, and gender in academe: Strangers in the tower?* New York: The Modern Language Association of America.

hooks, b. (1994). *Teaching to transgress: Education as the practice of freedom.* New York: Routledge.

Howell A. & Tuitt, F. (2003). *Race and higher education: Rethinking pedagogy in the diverse college classrooms.* Cambridge: Harvard University Press.

Illinois Board of Higher Education. (2003). *Report to the governor and general assembly on underrepresented groups in Illinois higher education.* Springfield: State of Illinois.

Illinois State University. (2008a). Educating Illinois. Retrieved from http://www.educatingillinois.ilstu.edu .

Illinois State University. (2008b). *Illinois State University Factbook.* Normal: Planning and Institutional Research.

Jackson, S. & Solis Jordan, J. (1999). *I've got a story to tell: Identity and place in the academy.* New York: Peter Lang.

Jacobs. L., Cintron J., & Canton, C.E. (2002). *The politics of survival in academia: Narratives of inequity, resilience, and success.* Lanham, MD: Rowman & Littlefield.

Knowles, M.F. & Harleston, B.W. (1997). *Achieving diversity in the professoriate: Challenges and opportunities.* Washington, DC: American Council on Education.

Li, G. & Beckett, G.H. (2006). *'Strangers' of the academy: Asian women scholars in higher education.* Sterling, VA: Stylus.

Maher, F. & Tetreault, M.K.T. (2007). *Privilege and diversity in the academy.* New York: Routledge.

Meyer, B. (1984). Minority group: An ideological formulation. *Social*

Problems, 32(1), 1–15.

Mohanty, C.T. (2003). *Feminism without borders: Decolonizing theory, practicing solidarity.* Durham: Duke University Press.

Morales, A.L. & Morales, R. (1986). *Getting home alive.* Ithaca, NY: Firebrands.

Nieves-Squires, S. (1991). *Hispanic women: Making their presence on campus less tenuous.* Washington, DC: Association of American Colleges and Universities. (ERIC Document Reproduction Services No. ED 334907).

Segura, D. (2003). Navigating between two worlds: The labyrinth of Chicana intellectual production in the academy. *Journal of Black Studies, 34*(1), 28–51.

Stanley, C. A. (2006). *Faculty of color: Teaching in predominantly White colleges and universities.* Bolton, MA: Anker Publishing.

Tack, M., & Patitu, C.L. (1992). *Faculty job satisfaction: Women and minorities in peril. (*ASHE-ERIC Higher Education Report No. 4).

Washington, DC: The George Washington University School of Education and Human Development. (ERIC Reproduction Service No. 355859).

Takaki, R. (1993). *A different mirror.* Boston: Little, Brown and Company.

Toro-Morn, M. (1995). Gender, class, family, and migration: Puerto Rican women in Chicago. *Gender and Society, 9*(6), 706–720.

Toro-Morn, M. (1999). Género, trabajo y migración: Las empleadas domésticas puertorriqueñas en Chicago. *Revista de Ciencias Sociales,* 7(June), 102–125.

Toro-Morn, M. & Alicea, M. (2003). Gendered geographies of home: Mapping second and third generation Puerto Ricans' sense of home." In P. Hondagneu-Sotelo (Ed.), *Gender and U.S. immigration: Contemporary trends.* (pp. 194–214). Berkeley: University of California Press.

Toro-Morn, M. (2004). The family in Puerto Rico: Colonialism, industrialization, and migration." In B. N. Adams & Trost J. (Eds.), *Handbook of world families*, (pp. 440–463). Thousand Oaks, CA: Sage Publications.

Toro-Morn, M. (2005). *Boricuas en Chicago*: Gender and class in the migration and settlement of Puerto Ricans in Chicago. In V. Vazquez and C.T. Whalen (Eds.), *The Puerto Rican diaspora: Historical perspectives* (pp. 128–150). Philadelphia: Temple University Press.

U.S. Census Bureau. (2009). The 2009 statistical abstract: The national data book. Washington, D.C.: U.S. Government Printing Office.

U.S. Department of Education, National Center for Education Statistics. (2009). *Digest of Educational Statistics,* 2008 (NCES 2009-020). Retrieved from http://nces.ed.gov/fastfacts/display.asp?id=61

Vazquez, J. (1992). Embattled scholars in the academy: A shared odyssey. *Callaloo, 15*(4), 1039–1051.

Villanueva, V. (1993). *Bootstraps: From an American academic of color*. Urbana: National Council of Teachers of English.

Wall, S. (2008). Easier said than done: Writing and autoethnography. *International Journal of Qualitative Methods, 7*(1), 38–52.

Winant, H. (2000). Race and race theory. *Annual Review of Sociology,* 26, 169–185.

CHAPTER FIVE

"Are We Change Agents or Pawns?"
Reflecting on the Experiences of Three African American Junior Faculty

*Michelle L. Jay, Catherine L. Packer-William,
and Tambra O. Jackson*

Abstract

This chapter reflects an on-going effort to use autoethnography as a medium to understand, analyze, and make meaning of the experiences of three African American female junior faculty members working in a predominantly White institution. Drawing on data that include in-depth phenomenological interviews, reflection journals, formal/informal dialogues, and official documentation, we explore a notable predicament that occurred during our second year in the academy and its subsequent impact on our professional and personal identities as well as our day-to-day existence within the college. The dilemma, which is detailed in a narrative format, highlights the conflicts that inevitably result from the daily negotiation between our self-imposed identities as scholar/activists and thus, "change agents," and the "agents of change" identity imposed upon us by our colleagues and administration.

With the conference less than 48 hours away, I decide that I've procrastinated long enough. I force myself into the chair in my office, open my computer, and command Word to open the three documents around which my presentation is based. As I scan the first title, "College Diversity Task Force: Recommendations for Addressing Equity and Fairness in the APR/T&P Process," my anxiety level begins to rise. Given that this is likely the thirty-second time that I've read this particular piece, the fact that it still has such an effect on me is simultaneously amusing and sad. It's amazing how much power the written word can have over our lives, and in this particular case, over my future in the academy—thus the anxiousness. In the dim light provided by my desk lamp, I scrutinize every line. As usual, I'm drawn to three particular passages. The first is the opening:

> *The Diversity Task Force (DTF) was appointed by the Dean of the College in January 2008 to develop recommendations for creating a more supportive and fair Annual Performance Review (APR)/Tenure & Promotion (T&P) process for faculty of color (faculty from historically underrepresented ethnic/racial groups). The creation of the DTF grew out of recognition of the vital contribution made by faculty of color to College programs, to academic and professional literature, and to a rich, vibrant, and critical culture within the College. However, university statistics reveal a disproportionately low number of faculty of color, particularly at full professor rank, in the College and in the University as a whole.*

A little further down the page:

> *The College has attracted a number of exemplary scholars of color in the past several years, and it is important that we not only strive to increase this number, but also to take actions that support their success and interest in continuing their careers here. These actions include nurturing an inclusive culture at the College and ensuring that faculty of color are supported through fair and equitable APR/T&P processes.*

And, at the bottom:

The DTF recognizes that issues of fairness and equity in the APR/T&P process can be problematic for all faculty members, but that these issues are compounded for faculty of color in predominantly White institutions and further compounded for women faculty of color. Therefore, it is critical for the College to ensure that the APR/T&P process addresses these issues and ensures greater equity and fairness for faculty of color.

I sit back from my computer, close my eyes, and breathe. Not my usual breath, but the kind of deep, intentional breathing that they teach in yoga classes—the kind that is intended to help you be "present," and "mindful." Unfortunately, in this particular moment, being present and mindful means allowing myself to feel things I'd rather not feel and to acknowledge things that I'd rather forget. I try to resist the urge to spend the next ten minutes processing, analyzing, scrutinizing, and re-analyzing what is, for me, the most important aspect of this document: the "faculty of color" that they are referring to is me. It's me! "Breathe," I tell myself, "just breathe."

I open my eyes slowly, close the "Recommendations" and stare at the second document. This one, which has come to be known in the college as "the white paper," is the catalyst of important change that's been occurring as of late (including the creation of the DTF and their subsequent recommendations). And, as luck would have it, I am one of its authors (along with Catherine and Tambra, my two closest colleagues who are also African American). We tend to refer to the document as "the policy statement" because when we were asked by Deanna, a college leader, to write it, she said "draft a policy statement." So we did, and here it is. And because we did, there have been consequences.

On the days when I am able to look at the policy statement without wanting to scream or cry (today is NOT one of those days), I'm quite proud of it. The language is eloquent, yet straightforward; academic, but not confusing. Moreover, the arguments it puts forth are backed up by 30 years of research on the lived experience of faculty of color in the academy. I'm particularly fond of its opening:

> *Faculty of color often have very different experiences navigating the academy than their White peers. The complexities of such experiences are further compounded by the context of a traditionally White institution. Indeed, as Allen et al. (2000) note, "elite racism" in the academy operates when the academic experience of professors of color (e.g., fewer mentors, different paradigms, lack of faculty members of color confers excessive race committee work and counseling of students of color, the debilitating effect of racism in the workplace, etc.) is overlooked. Further, the courts have recognized that the subjective nature of academic personnel evaluation decisions can create the potential for race, gender, and other illegal forms of discrimination (Leap, 1995). Thus, in an effort to create a climate where discrimination does not exist in the Annual Performance Review process, it is important to be aware of factors that can and have led to the creation of inequalities for faculty of color in higher education.*

I continue to read closely and am somewhat amazed at how much the challenges we document in the statement have manifested themselves in our own lives. "No," I think to myself, "we weren't crazy and we weren't being paranoid." All of this crap has actually happened...is happening! As a matter of fact, the evidence is lying next to my computer. I glance down at my third-year review and wish like hell that the shredder in our program office was functioning. I glare at the committee's comments on my service:

> *Dr. Jay has established a strong record of service. The APR committee is aware that our African American faculty members are asked to participate in multiple service activities in the Department, College and University. Nevertheless, we recommend that in the immediate future, Dr. Jay reduce those service activities to better prepare for her application for tenure and promotion.*

I know for a fact that the comments on Catherine's and Tambra's reviews were nearly identical to mine. "Don't these people realize that if even one of us reduced the service we're involved in, the college couldn't claim to be doing a damn thing related to diversity," I fume. "And our graduate students of color could forget about mentoring. The college's supposed commitment to diversity rides on the very service WE PROVIDE." "I've got an idea," I mutter, "Instead of patting us on the back for our service with one hand while simultaneously slapping us across the face with the other, how about we include a visible commitment to diversity and equity in the criteria used to evaluate faculty for APR and T&P. I'm quite certain your ratings would be deplorable." Mentally exhausted, I close the third document on the screen without even reading it. It's the narrative that I created last year as part of an authoethnographic writing exercise I engaged in an attempt to make sense of the ill-fated meeting with Deanna that led to the creation of the damn policy statement/"white paper" as well as her sketchy public stance on diversity. "I don't need to read the narrative," I tell myself. I can recite it in my sleep.

I get out of my chair and sit on the floor, reflecting on the first two documents and how the experiences of the women of color referenced in them aren't abstractions. They are **not** the experiences of the women of color research participants in the peer-refereed journal articles we constantly reference to validate our own experiences. They are *our experiences*—Catherine's, Tambra's and mine. I acknowledge once again, despite the simultaneous joy and terror it brings, that were it not for the three of us, those documents wouldn't exist. It is because of actions that we took, actions inspired by a shared desire to succeed (here success is defined by securing tenure and promotion), and an even stronger desire to bring about needed change in the process, that they do exist. Better still, they are at this very moment changing the college in ways we never imagined. The sheer irony of it all is overwhelming. I need to lie down.

I stare up at the ceiling, consumed by a realization that has haunted me for the last eight months: either we have actually facilitated institutional change that may actually benefit those who will come after us, or our activism will be used against us by White senior faculty members who are quietly biding their time until they can sit on our tenure review committee and shatter our dreams.

I sit back up and sigh. Not being able to see into the future, to see the consequences of our actions, really sucks. The more I think about it, the angrier and more frustrated I become. I'm pissed at myself, pissed at my colleagues, pissed at the college, and pissed at the world. "Why do I care about these clueless folks and what they think of me? They wouldn't know equity or social justice if it slapped them in the face? Why? Why? Why?" I get off the floor with an attitude, shut down my computer, and allow my thoughts to shift to the 'debriefing session' with Catherine and Tambra that I need to leave for in 5 minutes. Our sessions have become one of the few things that keep me sane since we started our careers here three years ago. I pack my things and shut the door. Walking down the hall, I decide that the caramel macchiato I'm planning to have will not be strong enough to help me forget this place, forget those documents, ease my anger, or relieve the nagging sense of pending doom that's crept into my chest. I dial Tambra on the cell and inquire as to whether we can "upgrade" our coffees for martinis. "That kind of day?" she inquires. I exhale and respond, "Aren't they all?"

Our Story

This chapter was written for the purposes of telling—truth-telling to be exact. The telling includes a re-telling of a narrative that I (Michelle) wrote about our experiences. The story presented in the next section (referred to as "the narrative") is based on our lived experience of an event that has, in many ways real and imagined, come to define our last two years as African American women junior faculty in our college. The story is about a meeting that occurred between us and Deanna, a college administrator, in August of 2007 and about subsequent salient events that have since occurred as a result of that meeting. Most important, however, the chapter includes each of our reflections on these events and thus contributes to our on-going efforts to process and make sense/meaning of what has transpired. Before sharing the narrative and our reflections on its implications, some contextualization and a brief explanation of how the story came to be documented is necessary.

Given the relative push to diversify the academy, institutions seem to be diligently attempting to increase their numbers of faculty of color without attending to the hostile environments we are invited to enter. Further, administrators often hire new faculty of color hoping that they will become a catalyst of/for change in their institutions while consciously or unconsciously ignoring the ways in which the burden of being "change agents" often puts us, as junior faculty, in professional jeopardy. The experience of being a new faculty member, with or without the "change agent" expectation, is even more daunting when one is both female and of color.

By and large, the experiences that we have had over the past three years as junior faculty are similar to those of other women faculty of color who teach in predominantly White institutions. Obliged to uphold the academy's "holy trinity"—research, teaching, and service – we, like our fellow colleagues of color, continue to try to strike a balance between the three and yet are often left feeling as though we aren't doing justice to any of them. Moreover, having been educated and trained in PWIs, we were well aware of the unique challenges that faculty of color, and in particular women of color, face in each of the three areas.

We were no strangers to the likelihood that our identities as educated Black females would lead to strife in the classroom and that students would use the power of the pen, via course evaluation, to express their unhappiness with being "forced" to consciously interrogate the functions of race, culture or language in educational contexts. We knew that our scholarship may be viewed as "race-based," and thus devalued, and that the master narrative (Stanley, 2007) would likely stand in the way of publishing our scholarship at the same rate of our White peers, whose work is often perceived to be "less controversial" and "more rigorous" because it is wholly devoid of anything that might make its reader uncomfortable. And we knew with utter certainty that, despite our best efforts to contain the boundaries of our service, we would be called upon to "serve" in ways that are never expected of our White colleagues, and thus, service would consume the precious time needed to produce our scholarship. All of this we knew.

It is what we did not know—what we could not have known prior to meeting each other and beginning our careers in the college—that would come to define the last three years for us. The first is that we would be part of a hiring cohort of 13 faculty members that included three African American women (us) and two Latinas who were on the tenure track, two additional African American female clinical faculty, and a White woman who would become a trusted ally. In short order, a peer mentoring group developed of which the three of us were a part. Consequently, the relationships that have developed between us, despite our disciplinary differences, have shaped our experiences. We have come to know and understand the academy in ways very different from those of our colleagues who are "the only faculty members of color" in their program or department or their college, etc. In a very real sense, we've never been alone on this journey. Having our own sisterhood has altered the ways we have experienced being women of color in the academy.

Second, we could not have known (though based on our shared racial background, we may have anticipated) that we would share a vision of the "service" as a mechanism for empowering our students, our communities, and ourselves. Indeed our conceptualization of service is consistent with Baez (2000) who argues that service can be a form of "critical agency" which might be used to "redefine institutional structures" (p. 364). We could not have anticipated the way in which our mutual desire to ensure each other's success (in a profession where many of us have fallen victim to the revolving door) would collide with our commitment to intentionally align our service with "race work." Nor that those two desires, combined with our shared identities as scholar/activist deeply committed to social and racial justice, would ignite our activism and aim it directly toward the college in an effort to change the very institutional structures that, in many ways, were set up to ensure our failure.

Yet, that is exactly what happened. And the consequences have been what Catherine calls, "psychological traumas which are beginning to manifest themselves physically." So this why my hair is falling out? Fabulous.

Capturing Our Story

> ...education, as a practice of freedom, requires educators to become self-actualized, and to reflect critically on one's own practice in order to understand one's role as an educator. This is particularly important for African American female scholars who are marginalized by institutional racism and sexism in the academy because the process enables them to think critically about the role these forces play in their lives as educators (Myers, 2002). As hooks (1994) observed through this self-actualization process, African American female educators may "develop important strategies for survival and resistance that need to be shared within black communities" (p. 118). (Fries-Britt & Turner-Kelly, 2005, p. 222).

As part of our efforts to support and sustain one another as well as to explore and understand our developing professional and personal identities as Black women in the academy, we decided to document our experiences. Realizing the uniqueness of our good fortune to be hired in a "cohort," we reasoned that capturing our experience might be useful, particularly in terms of helping us to process, understand, and potentially resolve the challenges we knew we were going to experience as Black women in a predominantly White university in the South.

Consistent with autoethnographic methodology in which data collection consists of, "multiple experiential and observation activities, analyzed through the researcher's identification of patterns and relationships implicit in the life of the community" (Reda, 2007, p. 178), this chapter draws on data generated from personal journals, official documents, informal and formal dialogues, and from in-depth phenomenological interviews wherein we interviewed each other as we attempted to make sense of the ways in which our day-to-day experiences in the academy are raced, gendered, and classed (Ellis, 2004). We chose to document our experiences using autoethnographic methods because, as Fries-Britt & Turner-Kelly (2005) note, autoethnography, specifically scholarly personal narrative, is "situated in Black feminist thought which accepts and encourages researchers to situate themselves within their scholarship" (p. 224).

This chapter represents part of our on-going attempt to craft a unique narrative argument, grounded in lived experience, which breaks from traditional academic discourse in an effort to communicate experiences that have otherwise been marginalized. If, as we believe, the crafting of autoethnographic representations can indeed be a form of activism in and of themselves, then we hope this chapter adds to the body of literature that explores the ways in which scholars attempt to create just, equitable environments within the academy for one another (Fries-Britt & Turner-Kelly, 2005; Danley & Green, 2004).

This chapter stands as a testament to our on-going attempts to create a just, caring and psychological safe space for each other.

The Narrative

"I'll be damned if the College is going to be the University's poster child for diversity." (Deanna, College of Education Faculty Meeting, April 29, 2008)

Language largely defines the possibilities of thought and action, so organizations use their institutional language to construct their structural identity and self-image…. (Rangasamy, 2004, p. 29)

"Poster Children"—April 2008

The day after our last faculty meeting in April of 2008, I shot an email to six of my girlfriend-colleagues (four African American women, one Latina, and a White ally). I needed to make sure that I had, in fact, heard what I thought I had heard during the meeting. If my recollection was correct, I was definitely going to need one of our group debriefing sessions. "Did she actually say, 'I'll be damned if the college is going to be the University's poster child for diversity'?" I asked. "Not only did she say it," one of them replied, "but did you catch the attitude that accompanied it?" Thus began one of our frequent, day-long, email dialogues about our college's commitment (or more accurately lack thereof) to diversity and social justice.

The comment that had inspired our flurry of emails had been made by Deanna, a college administrator, during the last faculty meeting of the year as a part her remarks on the recommendations of the college's Diversity Task Force (the first in the college's history) on *creating a more supportive and fair APR/T&P process for faculty of color*. I had been dreading the meeting because the presentation of the Task Force's recommendations (and the very explicit discussion about race and the APR/T&P process that was sure to follow) was the end result of an encounter that Catherine, Tambra and I had had with Deanna months ago. As I looked up at the large screen in the auditorium on which the recommendations had been projected, I knew that I should have been proud. I should have been beaming with the knowledge that the college might forever be changed (for the better) because of our efforts. Instead, all I could think about was a comment Catherine had made earlier that year when I had interviewed her for our research project. In reflecting on how "managing whiteness" and White people is one of the most salient factors of her day-to-day existence as a Black woman professor, she offered a rule that she has come to live by. "Once you've made White folks uncomfortable," she said, "you've lost!"

As Deanna began her review of the recommendations, I looked out across an auditorium **full** of White folks, shifting uncomfortably in their seats, and I knew with utter certainty that we were about to lose—*big time*.

"Policy Makers?"

Nine months ago, at the beginning of the year, Catherine, Tambra, and I had decided that, in an effort to prevent our falling victim to the college's "revolving door" when it came to faculty of color, thus becoming "poster children" of a different sort, we would have to be proactive. And proactive in this case meant taking our concerns directly to the administration. Indeed, given the generally positive 'vibe' that we had all gotten from them during our job interviews and the apparent delight they displayed with the "needed change" we represented, we had decided to explore the possibility of 'educating' them into allies. Our reasoning, flawed as it may have been, was that if we could raise their consciousness regarding our experiences as faculty of color in the academy, then there was a possibility that they might become informed advocates. And if we made them aware of the challenges we anticipated facing as Black women professors in the coming years regarding our scholarship, teaching, and service, and if we supported our concerns with the 30 years of research literature that documents those challenges, and if we linked those challenges to other faculty of color they may have worked with during their administrative careers, then we might have an enhanced shot at tenure. To be sure, we were not looking for handouts or asking that the criteria be altered for us. Rather, through bringing them into 'the know' so to speak, we reasoned that we could position them to become sources of support, rather than obstacles, should anything unfortunate happen on our journey to tenure…or at least to third-year review.

Today, I wonder, if given the chance to do it all over again, whether or not we would have had asked for that meeting. We left Deanna's office that day, our concerns having been affirmed, feeling as though we may be on the road to accomplishing our mission. What we didn't anticipate, however, was that we would also leave with the charge of drafting a "policy statement" that articulated the very issues we had come to discuss. As I look back, I can still see the dumbfounded expressions on our faces as we walked out the door. A policy statement? What the hell were three overburdened junior faculty members of color doing drafting policy? We just wanted to have a conversation…raise a little consciousness, not leave with more responsibility. "I thought we had just made it perfectly clear that we had too much to do as it is. And now you want us to do your job? Unbelievable!" I had mused. But were we in a position to say no? Of course not! When administrators (powerful White folk) ask you (young, untenured Black females) to do something, objecting is professional suicide. You smile, nod enthusiastically, and do what's asked of you…so we did.

Had we known that our policy statement would set off a series of events that has undoubtedly altered our own professional lives (for better or for worse), and likely those of faculty of color who will come after us, would we still have written it? Had we known that the statement would inevitably solidify our image as "change agents" (read: trouble makers) appreciated by some, and despised by who knows how many, would we still have done it? Had we known that, over the course of the year, the statement would be read by a number of people including the entire Administrative Council and would later lead to the creation of a college-wide Diversity Task Force charged with "developing recommendations for addressing equity and fairness in the APR/T&P process," and that the Task Force would come to be viewed by many White faculty as "unnecessary," silly," and "divisive," would we have opened our mouths?

I've given all of these questions a great deal of thought. And I've concluded that the more important question is, "Had Deanna known that day that her practice of "doing by delegating," (i.e. asking us to draft the policy statement) would come back to haunt her in ways she never imagined, would she still have suggested it?"

"Super Heroes"

Sitting in that faculty meeting, I was positive that people were staring at me. "Is it hot in here or is it just me," I wondered. As a person of color in a predominantly White setting, I'm quite familiar with feeling 'hyper-visible.' But as Deanna began addressing the Task Force's recommendations and a Q & A session ensued, I felt like an ant under a magnifying glass. Surely it's not that uncommon to have a public conversation about diversity and racial inequalities in a college, but when everyone in the room knows that the conversation is clearly about *you*, and is occurring *because of you*, that's a completely different ball game.

As I scanned the room, I tried to imagine exactly how many of my White colleagues were ticked off—angry that this was a topic of discussion, angry that race was being openly marked, and angry that, from their privileged point of view, this was not a conversation about fairness but about favoritism and exceptionalism, and that three new African American female junior faculty "upstarts" were to blame for it all. Who in the hell did we think we were anyway? As I sat there in my seat in the back row of the auditorium—a seat I had purposely selected in an effort to minimize my visibility to others (and had gotten there early to secure)—I knew who I wished I were—someone with the power to disappear on command.

"Would Be Firefighters"

The more I think about it, the more I believe Deanna indeed regrets that she asked us to draft that statement. In fact, my assessment is supported by my colleagues' and my own recollections of her statements during the meeting. While addressing the recommendations submitted to her by the Task Force, an African American female faculty member asked her for clarification on the college's position regarding diversity. Visibly irritated, she'd responded that she'd "be damned" if the college was going to be the university's "poster child for diversity." "We're not going to be the only game in town," she asserted and then proceeded to mount an argument as to why the university, not the college, should be responsible for implementing some of the Task Force's recommendations. Her remarks set the tone for the next 25 minutes of discussion and debate.

Why, I wondered, had she not chosen to contextualize her remarks in language that demonstrated the college's commitment to faculty of color and to larger issues of social justice and diversity in the college? Why had she not taken the opportunity to position the efforts made that year by Task Force members and other faculty organizations within the college to engage in open and frank conversations about the role of race and White privilege as important springboards towards positive change or to promote those efforts as having empowered the college to take a leadership role with regard to racial and social justice in the university?

I tuned out much of the remaining conversation, trying to reconcile her words with the college's mission statement, which expressly states our responsibility for being a leader for social justice! I suppose I shouldn't have been surprised, or angry, but I was. As I saw it, a tide of change that had been building in the college all year long had been effectively neutralized in five seconds flat. "While I agree that the university needs to get on the ball too," I fumed in my email to the girls the following day, "why should the college have to **wait** for the university to 'lead the way'?" "If Deanna's office was on fire, would she watch it burn while she waited on 'the university' to come put it out, or would she grab the extinguisher outside her office door and get to work?"

"Well, we can't be sure" one my colleagues replied. "After all, she is a delegator, not a doer!"

Later, Tambra wrote, "I was sitting there thinking that that was a really crappy thing to say, given that 20 minutes earlier, she had informed us that the college had a serious budget deficit. So, here we are in a room full of people worried about their jobs and pissed about not getting salary raises, and she has to go and say some nonsense like that! Thanks, once again, for connecting my presence, my issues, and my needs with White folks' money." Tambra was referencing the rumors (which we had addressed in our meeting with Deanna) being spread by some of our White colleagues that they weren't getting raises because the money for those raises was being used to hire faculty of color.

"Change Agents or Pawns?"

If we had had the foresight to see the ramifications of our meeting with Deanna, would we have gone in or taken our chances? I can't answer for Catherine and Tambra, but for me, the answer is yes—a tortured and conflicted yes, but a yes nonetheless. Indeed, as a womanist, I see little distinction between "academic" and "activist." If my professional efforts do not work towards improving the material realities for people of color, then I serve no real purpose. Period. And, Catherine, Tambra and I had long since determined that if we wanted careers working for racial and social justice as activists-scholars, we were going to have to fight for it. Given the "revolving doors" that are continually spinning at predominantly White institutions, it would be naïve of us to think that we couldn't become statistics as well. I (we) did what I (we) thought was right and, despite the backlash, despite the enemies I've surely made, I'd do it again.

But I'd be lying if I didn't also acknowledge that I often wake up in the middle of the night wondering if the very activism that sustains me, that makes putting up with all of the other b.s. is worth it, will be the one thing that stands between me and tenure. If I'm not here to continue the work that I've started, then I've failed. And I'm haunted by the possibility that if I am pushed (or walk on my own accord) through that revolving door, I *will never stop spinning*.

Another Debriefing Session

I meet up with Catherine and Tambra at The Wine Bar. It's been a year since the Diversity Task Force made its recommendations and our conversation, amongst other items, has turned to our assessment of the implementation (or in this case, lack thereof) of those recommendations. The Task Force's list had included four items, the first of which was: *supporting faculty of color with respect to APR/T&P*. Here they had suggested a professional development workshop to "sensitize all faculty members and administrators to known barriers to success for faculty of color in the evaluation process." They also suggested adding a "diversity representative" to APR and T&P committees. A third component to this recommendation included "an annual workshop for administrators, department chairs, APR/T&P chairs, and faculty members in each department." Faculty members who participated in this annual workshop would volunteer to act as diversity representatives. The three other recommendations included: *a) the immediate recruitment and hiring of senior scholars of color; b) the creation of a standing committee on diversity and; c) the development and implementation of a strategic action plan for diversity.*

To our knowledge, only Tambra's department appointed a diversity representative to their APR committee. And since no professional development or annual workshops had taken place, the representative had not been trained. On the upside, the current diversity committee, which took up this year where the Task Force had left off, had recently informed the college of its desire to apply for "standing committee" status, which requires a vote by the entire faculty. That vote will take place in the fall. If the committee is successful in accomplishing their goal, they will largely be responsible for the development of the strategic plan for diversity.

No senior scholars of color have being hired. Instead, two of the few tenured White allies in the college left this past winter. And we'll be attending a going-away brunch for the White junior faculty member/ally/colleague/friend whom we adopted into our sisterhood. It is my opinion that genuine White allies like her are treated as poorly in our college as faculty of color. A critical whiteness scholar, she too has had her research dismissed by her department colleagues as "not rigorous," her courses subjected to severe scrutiny and extensive approval processes not required of others in her department, and was accused of "experimenting" on her students by using texts that explicitly address race and racism. Further, in her interactions with White colleagues in her department, she was frequently forced into the position of "taking sides" along racial lines, asked to collude with them by acting as "an insider" in order to prevent "them" (her colleagues of color) from "running the place" and was often accused of being "unkind" and "unreasonable" when she interrupted racist thinking and remarks.

Realizing that I had never asked them directly, I turned to Tambra and Catherine and inquired, "If we had to do it all over again, would you still take that meeting with Deanna…knowing what we know now? In light of the fact that many of our colleagues resent us, fear us, and think that we're "upstarts," would you still meet with her and write that statement?

Tambra smiles and responds, "Yes! I would go in there again…standing on the shoulders of all those who stood before me and holding the hands of those who stand with me. And yes, I would go in there again…for all those who will come after me."

Nodding, Catherine concurs. She says, "I would still have the meeting…. but if I had to do it all over again, I would suggest that her asking us to come in there and solve a college issue for her by authoring that "white paper" is inappropriate. However, writing it ourselves does center us with power which is why we are feared and disliked for not "knowing our place." Plus, because we wrote that paper, it says exactly what WE needed it to say. As the only non-tenured African American faculty in the college, no one else could have our voice."

I reflect on their responses and nod my assent. Indeed, Tambra's sentiments match my own and are consistent with Baez's (2000) argument that faculty of color use their service as a mechanism to create change for others. And it is highly likely that the faculty of color who are hired after us will end up being the real beneficiaries of the changes that we have initiated. At the same time, as she pointed out, were it not for the faculty of color who came before us and paved the way, the three of us would not be here. My thoughts turn to Catherine's comments. I take a sip of my drink and turn to her.

"You are absolutely right," I said. "Had Deanna decided to write the statement herself or delegate it to someone who lacked our lived experience, or who was ignorant of the challenges that faculty of color face, things could be quite different right now. Perhaps she even recognized that much."

Catherine responds, "That three-page paper set off a domino effect of changes…half ass changes in some cases. However, WE are the ones to start the conversations—the good, bad, and ugly conversations—all of which need to be had. Damn, we even troubled the APR system! How powerful is that…although it may not work for us." Pausing for a moment she continues, "Of course, as the psychologist in the group, the piece that intrigues me the most is the psychological ramifications it has caused us—loss of hair (Michelle), gall bladder surgery (Tambra), and well with me…it's too tough to even speak the words right now. Not to mention the psychological unsafeness of it all…our wanting to hide and not be seen in the building, our increased lack of presence in the building because we work at home to feel safe, the effect on our relationships with colleagues…or the inability to have one. That is what interests me most. Can you say DEPRESSED?"

Indeed, I can. The psychological costs of our being Black women-change agents in the academy have certainly taken their toll. And, truth be told, there are days when I think it's all been worth it…and days when I am fairly certain that it's not. The days when I can clearly see the incredible value we add to the college, the worth we bring, and the righteousness of our work, are also the days when I am able to acknowledge a simple fact: the most vital unintended consequence of being Black women in the academy is that, by our very presence, we create change. We are agents of change in moments when it is our intention to be so, and perhaps more importantly, in moments when it is not. In reflecting on our identities as Black women in the academy, I've become much more aware of the choices we make about how we "present" ourselves as raced and gendered individuals. And I acknowledge that, too often, the choice is not ours to make. The only thing that we can do is hold true to who we are and to our commitment to create change, whatever the consequences may be.

For better or for worse, at all times, women of color in the academy are change agents. Catherine, Tambra, and I *are* agents of change. And if, as I believe, we have to negotiate the appropriation of our identities as change agents for political ends from time to time in order to facilitate that change, then so be it.

I raise my glass. "To us," I offer. They raise their glasses to meet mine. "To us!" we respond in unison.

References

Allen, W.R., Epps, E.G., Guillory, E.A., Suh, S.A., & Bonous-Hammarth, M. (2000). The Black academic: Faculty status among African Americans in US higher education. *The Journal of Negro Education, 69*(1–2), 112–127.

Baez, B. (2000). Race-related service and faculty of color: Conceptualizing agency in academe. *Higher Education, 39*(3), 363–391.

Danley, L., & Green, D. (2004). I know I've been changed: The impact of mentoring on scholarship. *National Association of Student Affairs Professionals Journal, 7*(1), 31–45.

Ellis, C. (2004). *The ethnographic I: A methodological novel about autoethnography.* Walnut Creek, CA: Alta Mira Press.

Fries-Britt, S., &Turner-Kelly, B. (2005). Retaining each other: Narratives of two African American women in the academy. *The Urban Review, 37*(3), 221–241.

hooks, b. (1994). *Teaching to transgress: Education as the practice of freedom.* New York: Routledge.

Leap, T.L. (1995). Tenure, discrimination, and African-American faculty. *Journal of Blacks in Higher Education, 7,* 103–105.

Myers, L. (2002). *A broken silence: Voices of African American women in the academy.* Westport, CT: Greenwood Publishing Group.

Rangasamy, J. (2004). Understanding institutional racism: reflections from linguistic anthropology. In I. Law, D. Phillips, & L. Turney (Eds.). *Institutional racism in higher education* (pp. 27–34). Sterling, VA: Tentham Books.

Reda, M. (2007) Authoethnography as research method? *Academic Exchange Quarterly , 11*(1),177–182.

Stanley, C. A. (2007). When counter narratives meet master narratives in the journal editorial-review process. *Educational Researcher, 36*(1), 14–24.

CHAPTER SIX

What Does Racism Look Like?
An Autoethnographical Examination of the Culture of Racism in Higher Education

Adah L. Ward Randolph

Abstract

This chapter examines the lived experiences of one tenured African American woman who has been a faculty member in colleges of education. It discusses the cultural context of higher education and how it either thwarts or supports racism in higher education from a critical authoethnographical framework. The data sources were analyzed through critical race theory and Black feminist theory. The author shares her experiences in hopes that they will alter institutional and individual practices in higher education.

Introduction

In my Introduction to Qualitative Research class, a student asked me, "What does racism look like?" At the time, it was an excellent question since this student, a White female, had been a witness to the racism I had experienced in my classroom. More importantly, she was willing to acknowledge it and talk about it with me. It was not the first time that I had encountered or experienced racism in the academy. In fact, I had come to expect it because it occurred so often that I was actually numb to it. Earlier in the class, another student,

Black and female, stated to me, "I could never be as calm as you are when students are being disrespectful. They never talk to the other professors in that way or question them the way they did you." At the time of this comment, I had learned to walk the tightrope and not fall off. Earlier in my career, it was not as easy (Ward Randolph, 2000). As a recently credentialed Ph.D. activist scholar, I had not been seasoned. I responded to her by saying, "Oh, I am used to it." It was in fact the first day of class, and I knew I was in for "one of those classes" where I am constantly questioned because I am African American *and* female.

Questioning had become part of the implicit curriculum in my classroom because I held a position of power as the "professor," but I was also a marginalized African American woman subject to differentials in power acquisition regardless of my professional credentials (Apple & Buras, 2006; Farmer & James, 1993; Pollard & Welch, 2006). I went home and wrote in my journal, "Why do I accept racism?" And more importantly, "Why has it become okay for students to speak through a racist lens at me the 'professor?'" These questions and experiences stand at the heart of this auto-ethnographical and historical research that questions the culture of the academy and my experiences in it. Moreover, it questions the academy rather than secondary or elementary education (Delgado, 2001; Foster, 1996; Lopez & Parker, 2003; Smith, Altbach, & Lomotey, 2002).

This auto-ethnographical research seeks to examine the following questions: 1) What are my experiences of racism in the academy? 2) How have my experiences of racism in the academy become "normal?" 3) How has a culture of racism been manifested and supported institutionally in the academy through human interactions, in meetings and in the classroom setting? 4) And finally, has the culture of racism changed in the academy? This research is grounded in history, higher education, critical race theory, the concept of cultural capital, and Black feminist theory (Collins, 2000; Farmer & James, 1993; Irvine, 2003; Lorde, 1984; Smith, 1980; Smith, Altbach, & Lomotey, 2002).

I contend that racism has historically been a major part of the foundation of our country. It is embedded in the taken-for-granted ways of thinking, talking, writing, and being that inhabit the institutions of this country. Higher education is no different. A majority of the research on Black women in the academy does not address the historical linkage of culture, race, class and gender in the academy with their experiences in the academy. This research is an exploration into one African American woman's experiences of racism in the academy grounded with the historical backdrop of desegregation of higher education and the impact of Black women within the academy as cultural beings. It builds upon past research in the field but departs in that it uses the self as the primary mode of understanding of the cultural milieu of higher education (Hull, Scott & Smith, 1982; Pollard & Welch, 2006; Vargas, 2002).

The qualitative analysis of the data sources is embedded in the culture of racism in higher education and cultural capital within that arena, and the intersection of the construction of race, class and gender, and my interactions within each of these spheres of influence in research (Delgado, 2001; Lopez & Parker, 2003; Parker, Deyhle, & Villenas, 1999; Pollard & Welch, 2006). Primary data sources utilized were the author's professional journal, letters of complaints, students, chairs, tenure and promotion evaluations, meeting minutes, and anecdotal musings. The secondary literature on higher education, Black women in the academy, Black feminist theory, women of color in the academy, cultural capital, and qualitative methodology are utilized in this research. Let me begin with a purposeful conception regarding critical ethnography and in turn, critical autoethnography.

Let's Talk About Methodology

When I first began this research, I thought about the need for me to question the culture of the academy. I thought about how the academy continues to support racism. I seek to **speak in a clear voice and a valid voice** about my experiences of racism as a professor in a predominantly White institution of higher learning. How would "my voice" be considered research? How would it be "validated" in the ivory tower? Thus, critical ethnography and autoethnography framed this research.

Critical ethnography "examines cultural systems of power, prestige, privilege, and authority in society" (Creswell, 2007, p. 241). Moreover, critical ethnography holds at its center an examination of "marginalized groups from different classes, races, and genders, with an aim of advocating for the needs of these participants" (Creswell, 2007, p. 241). This was my goal. However, I am not advocating for everyone because I cannot speak for everyone, but I can shed light on the experience of one African American woman within the cultural context of higher education: my experience. But there is more.

Creswell (2007) suggests that one wishing to "study themselves and their own experiences" (p. 123), should turn to autoethnography. I am illuminating my cultural experiences as a member of a higher education institution. Consequently, my research rests upon both of these frameworks, critical ethnography and autoethnography, and they both serve as the methodological basis for this chapter. Autoethnography can be defined as "an autobiographical genre of writing and research that displays multiple layers of consciousness, connecting the personal to the cultural" (Ellis & Bochner, 2000, p. 739). By utilizing these approaches to my research, I will be able to surmise some insights regarding the culture-sharing group that is existent in higher education and their core values and beliefs and how they work and relate to one African American female faculty member; I will describe my involvement in the subculture; and I will posit how I resist or maintain an oppositional culture to the one I am a part of (Creswell, 2007).

I am seeking my own emancipation by speaking truth to power through examining the culture and institutional structure I reside in as an academic. At the heart of the analyses are my unearthed pain, confusion, and misery. I never thought the academy would be like this. I thought being qualified was enough. Clearly, there is more required. I challenge the status quo of how things are done and expose them through my moments of resistance to "power, inequality, dominance, repression, hegemony and victimization" (Creswell, p. 70). In the words of Fannie Lou Hamer, "I'm sick and tired of being sick and tired" (Locke, 1993, p. 34) of the onslaught of slights, discrimination, and unmerited suffering I experience on a daily basis sometimes as a Black female faculty in a college of education. I challenge you to think differently as I present to you these moments of resistance to oppression and attempts to silence my cultured voice. I ask you to examine the discourse in complaints, evaluations, actions of the individuals and the institution.

The Beginning of Probation: Learning Coping Mechanisms

When I first began my work as a full-fledged, tenure-track faculty member at Syracuse University, I was told I "needed good evaluations" by one of the associate deans. At the time, I wondered what this meant, but, I heard the implicit message that I would be judged based on student views of my effectiveness. I thought, how can a subjective view speak to effectiveness? There have to be other measures. So, I set about developing interim evaluative measures for my courses to examine my teaching and student learning before the university's end of semester evaluation. I reasoned this would build another source of data for analysis of effectiveness. However, another query came to mind: Will students really see me, or will they see a distortion of me? I thought about the novels *Invisible Man* (Ellison, 1995) and *The Spook Who Sat by the Door* (Greenlee, 1969). When had these students seen African American female faculty members? Besides my one African American female colleague, there were no others like me, and she left after a year in the department. I was alone. But, as Anna Julia Cooper attests, as I entered the room, the "whole Negro race enters with me" (Lemert & Bahn, 1998, p. 63). I went into the classroom armed with knowledge and competence. What I found was that some would see this, others would not. I polled my class anonymously to see if any of them had ever had an African American professor. For many, I was their first. By the end of the semester, however, many of them had become my mentees. Some even went on to pursue their masters and Ph.D. Still, some students would see the spook. To others, I would be invisible and they treated me as such through their lack of eye contact. Not as the person of authority in the classroom but someone who was there because of Affirmative Action (Moody, 2004). The looks on the faces when I showed up at times were disheartening. The faces asked, "Is this our professor?" like in the classic book *Are You My Mother?* (Eastman, 1998), where the baby bird searches to find his mother who looks just like him. Is she the teaching assistant? Many of my students have passed me in the hall and thought I was just another student. They are literally in shock when I come in and write my name on the board, as if all of the air was suddenly sucked out of the room. They have to gasp for air until they can catch their breath, and the color of their skin returns to pale pink rather than various shades of red. This of course is not the response of all, but I have found that it takes only a few. So, I came up with this equation: 25 percent will love me, 25 percent will hate me and 50 percent will be in the middle. It calmed my nerves and quieted the looks of disbelief, particularly as I went over the syllabus. Eyes become wider because I believe in the power of knowledge and learning. Rigor is at the core of my courses. Is this my attempt to prove myself? Or is it just my intention to make my students competent? I reckon at some points in time, both of these intentions have been embedded in my course requirements (Moody, 2004). I am seeking to develop educators who are critical thinkers, who have a knowledge base from which to consciously educate their students to become critical thinkers as well as actors. Consequently, the banking model approach is not utilized in my courses (Freire, 2000; hooks, 1994). Still, I am the professor.

After a semester, I was supposed to alter the understandings about race, class and gender in a class primarily full of White folks. It is an impossible and improbable task. But I tried. It was how I began my teaching career in the academy—teaching the scorned and often-contested diversity classes. In the fall of 1998, after a student disagreed with my use of the term, "Jew," I had a complaint. Mind you, I had used the term "Jew" in the class before this date. More importantly, the book we used—Ronald Takaki's *A Different Mirror* (1993)—used the term as well. I subsequently learned from a supportive student that that was not the issue. My other colleague often used the term "Jew" in class as well, and *the same students* had no issue. So, what was the real problem? By the end of the semester, it had turned into a split class due to the student who now was not a single student but a group of hostile dissenters. Even though I had continued to try to resolve the issue with the (now two) students during the semester, it dragged on, and on and on, and I spent valuable time with the two students, the chair, and eventually with the associate dean to resolve their angst. In sum, the students requested that I change my writing assignments and decrease the degree and depth and breadth of them as well as extend their due dates. They wanted to be able to say the word "ouch" when we talked about difficult subjects. Based on my educational philosophy and belief in rigor, I did not change the requirements for the course which had been stipulated per contract the first day of class. They could, however, use whatever word they wanted to address their emotional/mental/psychological distress with difficult subjects. During the winter semester, the dean unexpectedly called me to his office. He had met with the students unbeknownst to me and rendered his verdict based on their complaint. I was held responsible by him based on the students' unquestioned testimony for the "split" that had developed in my class according to and because of them. I was responsible for their angst and actions rather than the students themselves. I had no knowledge of the student "split" until he mentioned it in his office. I knew that the two students attempted to alter the requirements, but I did not know that they had continued to canvas to the point of creating this "split." Many students disagreed with the students, and on one occasion in class when the two students attempted to thwart the learning process, a student disagreed with them and requested that they be about the business of learning the material. It was my first lesson about what it meant to be an African American woman teaching about "diversity" in a predominantly White institution (Delpit, 1996). I was guilty of a crime that I did not quite understand. Still, I was *guilty*. I never knew who my accusers were, but I knew who the ringleaders were. Afterwards, I learned from a student supporter that the mob actually canvassed against me in other classes, even calling other students. Yet, another student at the end of the semester presented me with my first gift from a student: a silver bracelet with the word "woman" written in several languages. She commended me for doing an excellent job. All was not lost. After the dean humiliated me in his office, they continued to protest. Clearly, I had not been their professor (Moody, 2004; Ward Randolph, 2000). They had seen the spook who sat by the door.

None of the institutional structures protected or fought for me as one of them. I was alone.

In the summer of 1999, I left Syracuse University, not because of the protest by students, but because of an opportunity to join my husband at another university. Still, the lessons I learned from the institutional milieu and how it supported the racism of students I never forgot (Ward Randolph, 2000). I took that armor into my diversity classes at Ohio University (OU). Since 2002, however, I have taught methodology courses. Has changing the content of the course changed how students view me? Has the move from a private to a public institution changed my experience of institutional policies and practices?

Recent Evaluations

Even though I now teach methodology courses the student responses have been based on the level of the student in this public institution. There is a clear difference between masters and doctoral students, that is, until recently. I have found that even though my curricular material has changed, I have not. I am still the only African American woman in my department and the only African American woman to ever receive tenure at my institution *in its history*. I thought that switching from teaching race, class and gender to teaching methodology would provide me with some psychological and emotional distance from trying to awaken an understanding of "isms" in preservice teachers; it had been an onerous task (Irvine, 2003; Popkewitz, 1998). At the master's level, I have not found this to be the case. Student contentions are no longer just about the subject matter, but their responses are more virulent regarding who I am as a person. On some level, I would argue that this was because I was expected to teach about race as the only Black woman in my college. It was acceptable to students even though they did not like the rigorous content I attached to it. But, methodology classes have proven to be sometimes even more personally confounding.

As noted earlier, my doctoral qualitative methodology class in the summer of 2006 led me down this road of examining the culture of racism, White supremacy and privilege in higher education. As I looked over my evaluations, the numeric evaluation was 3.86 on a scale of 5. It was the lowest numerical score *I had ever received* for this course. Generally, the quantitative evaluation represented what I often earned from master's level students in the Introduction to Research course. During the class, I had been interrupted when talking to a group of students, interrupted when answering questions, disrespected by talking when I or other students were engaged in learning. They questioned when I informed them when assignments were due. I experienced the shuffling of papers and the collecting of parcels before class was officially ended, and finally, was called a liar by a student when asked about my personal experience to which she replied, "BULL" in a very loud, antagonistic voice. Several students commented to me that they had never seen some of the students speak to, treat or act towards me as they did to other professors in the program. In other words, my colleagues, all White of both genders, had been granted their professional deference and authority and subsequent power. It was clear to the student, who asked me about racism, that she had witnessed these behaviors and more importantly, she knew of institutional occurrences where they were supported by my colleagues. But let me turn to the written comments on the evaluation.

One student wrote, "*weak teaching, hard to follow and sometimes unprofessional.*" The student continued "*I suggest she teach research classes, not educational classes.*" Yet, this same student wrote, "*She has a good knowledge base.*" What does this discourse mean? What were her/his expectations of me? On the other hand, another student wrote in regard to the strengths of the course, "*Honestly, the strength of the course* was the instructor. *Dr. Ward Randolph's strengths as a qualitative researcher, and her interest in our dissertation interests."* In regard to weaknesses, the student wrote," *No weaknesses; even though the course was very demanding, it was very rewarding."* This student closed by writing, *"I felt very fortunate to have taken this course face-to-face and not online. From what I heard about the online version of the course, the course should never be taught online."* The student cohort had a listserv. I was not privy to it. Only faculty and students in the program had access to it. It became a tool from which much confusion and misinformation would be "heard." I only became aware of the listserv the last day of class. Still, another student provided mixed results as well.

The student wrote, *"Professor—very knowledgeable in field. Assignments were directly related to course objectives."* Weaknesses were *"Comments were made by the professor that were derogatory to the doctoral program i.e., OU's doctoral program is not as rigorous as Ohio State's and she intended to make it rigorous. Another comment to the effect that an Ed.D. is not as good as a Ph.D. Graded papers counting off things that were missing in her eyes but not required according to the syllabus."* And in regard to improvement, *"Please refrain from derogatory comments about the program or degree. We were insulted."* **Aha, herein lies the rub!** What do these comments mean and how could students write that I knew my material but base their evaluation on "comments?" What is missing from this written comment? context and circumstance. Only a few students took the time to write written comments at all. But, this particular evaluative information explains the disparity between my numeric evaluations and the mixed qualitative data. I had not made a "comment" in class. *I was responding to a direct question.* My answer to the question offended them. And even though they had learned a great deal, they held my response, not comment, against me. According to Moody (2004), this is one of the disadvantages faculty of color face: continued penalization. I call it unmerited suffering. For further clarification, let me add just a bit more detail.

First, I was asked about the difference between an Ed.D. and a Ph.D. They are not the same degree. Everybody knows this or so I thought. One is a Doctor of Education while the other is a Doctor of Philosophy: hence, Ed.D. and Ph.D. Why was this disconcerting to students, particularly since the conversation and question were asked *the first day of class*? If I had known students were going to be "offended," and I would be penalized for my answer, I would not have answered the question asked which was, "What is the difference between a Ph.D. and an Ed.D.? I answered, "The Ed.D. is considered a practitioner's degree. A Ph.D. is considered a research degree. It is the highest degree you can obtain. It is higher than a M.D., which is why a M.D. that does research is often a Ph.D., M.D. This was my answer to the question. Some of the students' faces registered shock: they had thought they were viewed as the same within the academy. Still, my response was not a "comment" out of the blue. It was an answer to their question. How would my chair have known? She was part of the listerv. Furthermore, as I analyzed this student's concerns for improvement, what is wrong with rigorous? The program we offered was different from the one at Ohio State. It was a fact. Or was it the messenger rather than the message?

Having conducted research at Yale University, I know there is a difference between Yale and Ohio State. All institutions are known for different things. A graduate of such an institution like Yale has connections. It is a source of social, cultural and political capital. We fail in higher education to openly address how these systems of advantage and access work (Smith, Altbach, & Lomotey, 2002). When asked a direct question, I answered based on my knowledge of cultural, political and social capital in higher education. I had no idea it would become a bone of contention for students *and* my colleagues, one who was an Ivy graduate himself. I had not understood the rules of discourse around this issue at OU. Moody (2004) contends this is another disadvantage for faculty of color: "spending time deciphering the complex psychological dynamics unfolding between them and majority students or colleagues (p. 24)."

In my evaluation, the students focused on my "comment" which made explicit the taken-for-granted assumptions concerning doctoral degrees and rating criteria amongst institutions of higher education. My declaration of the hidden social and cultural milieu was viewed as "derogatory" so much so that five weeks later students punished me for speaking that truth. While they acknowledged my strength of knowledge and rigor, the students were not willing to support that contention completely and rationalized by discounting my teaching credibility amongst my peers.

My chair, a member of the cohort's primary teaching faculty, publicly reprimanded me through email concerning being "professional." We had had no conversations. Nor had she been in the classroom. She defended the program and thwarted my ability to foster a high quality learning environment. Through her actions, students were institutionally supported and utilized institutional structures to "put me in my place." I learned I was often a hot topic of conversation on the student listserv amongst the students and my colleagues who were both White (one male and one female), my chair, both liberals (Moody, 2004). Hence, I received lower evaluations not based on competence or actual student learning but their personal "insult." Do my colleagues recognize that my teaching evaluations are never just about how well I know the subject? My race, gender and culture are part of the equation, not to mention that I usually teach required courses. Since they never see the qualitative comments, how are my colleagues to decipher the effectiveness of the quantitative evaluations of my teaching? They base their evaluation of me on the number, not the context, the subject, or the multiplicity I hold as a racialized person in a predominantly White context. What I have found is that when one student is dissatisfied or feels disempowered, it can easily turn into a metaphorical "gang rape" or mob action resulting in power by force. This next experience explicates how the culture of the academy supports White supremacy and institutional racism in the name of protecting students.

Manchester: Violated by the Mob

During the winter quarter of 2006, I received a message from my chair concerning a letter she had received. I informed her that I would meet with her but not alone. I had learned from the Syracuse experience to never go to a meeting alone, particularly when you had no idea what it was about (Ward Randolph, 2000). I enlisted the support of Institutional Equity. When we arrived at her office, she indicated that she had a "complaint" regarding my overload teaching during the fall of 2005 at a branch campus and handed me a packet. Two months had passed since I had taught the Introduction to Research class to a special education master cohort. The first page of the packet was a letter from the associate dean of the branch campus dated December 12, 2005. It read:

> . . . I decided to send you this note about the complaints that I have received from students about a faculty member. . . .A member of Dr. Adah Ward Randolph's class called me and asked that I meet with her class to hear numerous complaints. Most of the class attended the discussion. There were a few very vocal students who had numerous complaints. They said that their grades were good and that they weren't concerned about themselves but for future students. There were a few defenders of Dr. Ward Randolph's approach. Unfortunately the defenders were Black while the complainants were Caucasian. All but one of the complainants praised Dr. Stein (a White professor in the department) for her approach, commending her for explaining her expectations and providing excellent feedback. One student disagreed with her ideas but felt it was an age difference issue.

He continued;

> The major complaints about Dr. Ward Randolph's class were:
>
> 1. Numerous absences.
> 2. Coming late to class and being unprepared.
> 3. Telling the class that she had priorities other than teaching the class.
> 4. At the end of class, dropped assignments (assignments previously required but eliminated by the professor), telling the class that this was what they wanted.
> 5. Poor guidance on projects, especially reflective papers.
> 6. No response to e-mails.
> 7. Poor feedback on assignments—didn't give helpful examples.
> 8. Seemed to have a chip on her shoulder rather than a passion for the subject.
>
> I am enclosing a copy of a written statement by one student who said she represented a number of students in the class. I appreciate your attention to this matter. I think that these were new graduate students who needed to understand what the expectations were for graduate students. (This is not just a regional campus issue!)

The only item that was true was I was late. However, this was because I could not get access to the printer on this campus until someone showed up—a student worker. This was a Saturday class and there was only one person on at the desk, who often was not there before the start of the day, which in turn made me late for class even though I had been on campus *before* class. And if I am running from one building to another after getting access to the printer and placing my materials in order of use, it looks like I am unprepared. But, I had not been unprepared with my subject material. Still, I would apologize to the students when this happened. But, the fact that I would apologize for a structural issue of no fault of my own did not come across in the complaint. Nor the conversation where I spoke about all of the things that a faculty member has to do besides teaching such as service and research in addition to teaching. Clearly, the student heard what she wanted to hear, not what I actually said nor the context in which it was said. Even recounting this makes me angry because I still feel like I have to prove my innocence while my guilt was assumed.

Again, one student had turned into an angry gang. This gang captured an opportunity to victimize me as a group, not as an individual. Did they feel powerless and sought to be empowered? Not one student had requested a meeting with me one-on-one. One particular student had loudly talked about her displeasure concerning their having to do a group assignment but I took it for what it was: her angst. What I did not understand is that she wanted me to change my criteria for the assignment, and to sooth her concerns by altering the chosen assignment. I believe that pre-service teachers need to experience teaching in a classroom as well as cooperating with their colleagues. Thus, the assignment is aimed at supporting students to become responsible for their own learning rather than employing the banking model (Freire, 2000). I did not change the assignment. Research classes, I believe, should not be taught using a banking model. Research is about discovery. Not about getting the "right answer." It is about thinking. Again, not one student had requested a meeting with me. Instead they went to the powers that be—directly.

One student had "called him." This meant that the students went to the trouble of finding out who they should contact. Why had they not gone to the coordinator of the program? Usually, students will ask questions of me in front of other students rather than see me in my office. I believe they feel safer this way. Am I, a Black woman, that intimidating? I contend that a student or students are attempting to coerce the class to see their view, thereby nullifying my position and power in hopes of having their way through numbers of students rather than allow their individual position to stand alone. What I did not understand was that from that moment on because I did not co-operate with the one particular student, every word I said, every action I took would be recorded as evidence against me. Everything I said and did not say would be taken out of context and circumstance, away from the classroom. It did not need to be placed in context nor did it even have to be the truth. It would serve as evidence of my incompetence. They went looking for it and found it through their racialized gaze (Caraway, 1991). From all indications, it was only a few of the students because many students, including two White male students in particular, made a point of thanking me for the course. One of the White male students had had my husband for public policy, and even though he thought my course was rigorous, he thought my husband's was harder. Moreover, at the actual meeting, the Black students had disagreed with the major complainer. More importantly, many students thanked me for providing them with a breadth and depth of assignments while one positive and vocal White student actually attempted to defend me against, as she called them, "the whiners" by emailing the associate dean when she heard what the few students were planning to do. Again, this was a Saturday course in which the majority of the students were non-traditional students and worked during the week at various occupations. The program was an alternative licensure program.

According to Clarke (2005), "through understanding the discursive constructions of implicated actors and 'actants,' analysts can grasp a lot about the social worlds and the arena in which they are active and some of the consequences of those actions for the less powerful" (p. 48). I am examining these actions and "actants" to do just that. What was the impact of this on me: the "less powerful?" Clarke (2005) contends that dominant discourses are "reinforced through extant institutional systems of law, media, medicine, education, and so on. A discourse is affected in disciplining practices that produce subjects/subjectivities through surveillance, and examination" (Clarke, p. 55). I had come under surveillance, and my actions were now being used against me without my knowledge as evidence of my "regulated freedom" (Clarke, p. 54). At the heart of my pseudo freedom was difference based upon beliefs about power. Foucault argues, "the gaze that emanates from a site of power and authority, (always already appropriating the right to look and to see, attempting to do so hegemonically,) and thereby invisibling/silencing other perspectives/gazes" (Clarke, p. 58). At the heart of students' produced verbal and written discourse was difference. And because I was different, as indicated from their comparison to my White female colleague, they produced this discourse by using "reactionary or passive, forces in the games of truth" (Clarke, p. 59) through their letter and meeting with the associate dean, and their harassment of one White female defender that I learned of on the last day of class. Differences such as race "influence how practice is practiced" (Clarke, p. 661). Students reacted utilizing unconscious power based on irrational fears to thwart my inclusion as a rational cultural being, as a different racial being, while not addressing the obvious difference: race. This was because of the significance of race and how individuals and institutions historically have been allowed to respond/react to its presence in places where it should not be (Irvine, 2003; Smith, Altbach & Lomotey, 2002). They went to the associate dean.

Now, the letter and its addendum from the associate dean went to the coordinator who sent it to the interim dean, both associate deans, and to my chair at the main campus. I was not part of the process until my chair contacted me. I was immediately put in the position of **proving** I had done nothing wrong without due process. I had been gang raped in the academy. It was *all about power and privilege.* In the four-page single-spaced comments, this is some of what the one student wrote as a "representative" of students in the class:

We are of the understanding that complaints have been made previously about Dr. Randolph, but she is still "teaching" this course. She may be proficient at doing research, but she cannot teach it. At every turn, by her words and actions, she clearly demonstrated her total disregard for the students and the course. We are not lazy students and do not expect to be "spoon-fed." However, there is a difference between cognitive dissonance and total frustration. Whatever we learned, we learned in spite of Dr. Randolph, not because of her. It is unconscionable that the University continues to employ her as an instructor.

They continued;

We implore you not to share this information with anyone, but especially, Dr. Randolph, until after she submits our grades for this course. We are positive that there would be reprisals. Obviously, we are not coming forth to help our class. Many people have advised us not to risk academic injury to ourselves. That we are taking this chance should demonstrate how seriously we consider that something must be done. Thank you for coming well after the close of your business day to hear our concerns.

I had turned into the "gila monster" a reptile, as my brother used to say or the *Monster from the Black Lagoon*, a 1954 monster movie that was reissued in the 1970s. I had become a specter, a distorted image from their racialized gaze. I, as difference, should not be there. It was "*unconscionable*" that I was employed by the university. They wanted me gone even with tenure. They utilized institutional support of the culture of racism and difference in the academy to speak to my incompetence without due process. Through comparison to their one other professor, they declared their preference: White and female. The students utilized their power as "*a group.*" This assured they *would be heard.* At the same time, I had been disempowered. I had been raped. It is important to note that this effort was spearheaded by an older White woman who consistently questioned my authority and disrespected me to the point of not even providing me, the pro-

fessor, with a copy of the presentation her group conducted (Caraway, 1991). I had to ask for it. Were they really concerned about other
students, their grades and the program? I would tender "no."

The students used innuendo and untruths to defame me. They
called upon institutional history concerning Blacks' place in the academy (Smith, Altbach & Lomotey, 2002). Mind you this was after Hur-
ricane Katrina struck New Orleans when images of Black people were
everywhere, none of them positive. We must examine the macro
structure outside the university when analyzing our experiences with
students. The White pre-service students, who had never taught,
knew what they needed and who could teach them (Irvine, 2003;
Popkewitz, 1998; Vargas, 2002). I, an African American woman, did
not understand what is real teaching given my history as a member of
a deficient group (Moody, 2004). *Yes, I could do research, but I could
not teach it*. The protestors saw me and questioned my teaching and
impact on their learning. They learned "in spite" of me. *But, they had
lied*. More importantly, the institutional leader/structure ran with it.
They believed them to be telling the truth. Why did they not question
the students? Why was I denied due process?

This experience reminded me of an incident at Syracuse where
two students became three then became six, then became twelve as
the original two complainers campaigned against me so much so that
even my own advisee doubted me, and a White male student, who
had not been to many classes, came to my office and told me that he
did not think I had the right to determine the content of the course. I
reported him to his advisor. Again, racism takes energy and it saps
the strength and energy of the raped. The rapist was supported by the
system. The raped has to prove she was.

After months of addressing this issue through meetings and letters, the associate dean responded on June 21, 2006. He wrote; "The
student assured me that those in the class had expressed their con-

cerns to you and had been rebuffed" (personal communication, December 12, 2005). He continued, "They said they were concerned about retaliation by you through their grades. I met with them and I was given a written list of complaints" (personal communication, December 5, 2005). In other words, **HE BELIEVED THEM**. He bought into racism and White supremacy exhibited by the students even when other students disagreed. But, I forgot, they were Black. But, I knew of a White female student who was harassed by the students for her stance against their razing. She too had written the associate dean. She had labeled the students "whiners." She too, like them, worked full-time and was even a single parent. Still, she chose to complete the work required in the course without complaint. The associate dean chose to ignore her. In a position of power that could have made all of the difference in my experience, he abused a faculty member and university policy. After all, I was Black and female. So, he believed them and felt that he *knew me* through the "few vocal students" that was enough for him. The fact that students spent time and energy to thwart my placement and standing as a tenured faculty member speaks to the conception of real diversity and the lack of attention paid to the students' behavior and actions and the rationale behind them. They were viewed as legitimate. I was the illegitimate one. Throughout their letter, they constantly compared me to a White female who had been at the University for over twenty years. I am sure her style of teaching was different from mine, but I learned from our conversation about these students that our philosophical stances about rigor were the same. Just my presence for some represents cognitive and cultural dissonance. Where in their lives have they had the opportunity to see a clear picture of what African Americans have to offer? In the academy, I am fighting distorted images and conceptions. It does not matter what I teach or where.

Delpit (1996) defines the "the culture of power" (p. 129). She contends that there are five tenets of this culture: Issues of power are enacted in classrooms. There are codes or rules for participating in power; that is, there is a "culture of power." The rules of the culture of power are a reflection of the rules of the culture of those who have power. If you are not already a participant in the culture of power, being told explicitly the rules of that culture makes acquiring power easier. And finally, those with power are frequently least aware of—or least willing to acknowledge—its existence. Also according to Delpit, those with less power are often most aware of its existence. Delpit (1996) further argues that "For many who consider themselves members of liberal or radical camps, acknowledging personal power and admitting participation in the culture of power is distinctly uncomfortable" (p. 131). In essence, "White educators had the authority to establish what was to be considered 'truth' regardless of the opinions of the people of color, and the latter were well aware of that fact" (Delpit, p. 131). The students had experienced "cultural dissonance" in our interactions in the classroom. The "cross-cultural interactions" were disconcerting to them so much so that they sought to have me removed from the university under the guise of protecting other students. The institutional structure supported their power and protected them from me. The institution participated in my vilification and condemnation. At no time were the students' contentions, intentions or lies questioned by anyone. I really was not a part of the structure of higher education. They took back their power. I still had to speak truth to power.

In *Faculty Diversity: Problems and Solutions* (2004), JoAnn Moody argues that minority faculty in majority institutions experience "extra taxes and burdens" (p. 12). African American faculty are always being evaluated, and their "qualifications and achievements are always suspect." Regardless of rank, African American faculty are on "perennial probation" (p. 13) and have "to prove themselves twice as accomplished as majority colleagues" (p. 13.) My dialogue in class was highly scrutinized. At no time, did I not feel like my colleague Nell Painter, who called her experience in the academy as "tiresome in the extreme" (p. 13). Hence, months later instead of working on my current teaching assignment, service requirements or research, I had to pause to think about my response to this new, but no different, onslaught.

After meeting my chair on February 2, 2006, I went home and wrote this in my journal: "Bending the Rules: My Experiences of Racism in the Academy."

> I was watching my favorite channel, HGTV, when I heard one of the artists on "I Want That," say, "You have to know what the rules are, before you can bend them." His reflection hit me like a ton of bricks as I thought about how many times I have experienced racism in the academy. After one scorching event, a good friend and mentor of mine, said to me, "They didn't make the rules for us. We were never supposed to be at the table. The rules were for them." When I combine these two concepts, it is clear to me why I continue to experience racism that my White colleagues have no indication about…. I am now clear that the rule does not apply to Black female faculty, and in this case to me when my due process is violated. Again, they know the rule of due process and probably would follow it for White faculty, male or female. But, for me…they know they can "bend it."

I went on to recount my first experiences of racism at my former institution where the institutional structure supported the students' racism (Randolph, 2000). The dean in that case indicated to me the difficulties I had experienced were not because of race but because of class, because he believed I had been raised "poor." It was his assumption. In my musings, I turned my attention to the Manchester complaint. I wrote:

> This past quarter, I had again, White female students, charge me with being an "uppity negro" who was in charge of their grade. Hence, they "feared"

coming to me…. It is only after "hearing" this comment that I know now
that the rules will never apply to me…. I know this for what this is. It is
RACISM…

I concluded that section by writing, "I am an uppity Negro because I am competent." I needed to let the anger out and let it go. I
knew I was judged by an unjust, different and higher standard.
Moody (2004) argues that minority faculty experience in addition to
the presumption that they are incompetent, nine other things ranging
from receiving little or no mentoring to representing their entire
group or being vulnerable to unfair evaluations of their worthiness
and their work. Whereas Moody (2004) details these ten struggles that
minority faculty will most likely have to overcome, a majority of these
were embedded in the students' complaint. Eventually, I did respond.

On March 25, 2006, I wrote to my chair, and addressed the three
most glaring fabrications by the students. I asserted "the students…
violated the university's commitment "to equitable treatment of all
members of the university community. Why? …I think the answer
resides with who I am, an African American woman." I concluded
that, "these students, however, disregarded university policy which
should have been brought to their attention and utilized university
structure to punish, harm, discredit, and violate a faculty member
…the student(s) violated academic honesty." I went on to ask for a
reprimand for the associate dean. Nothing ever came of it. My chair
supposedly had done her part. The interim dean acknowledged nothing. The damage was done.

Conclusion: What Can We Learn?

First, White supremacy embedded in the culture of the institution altered my acceptance and experience in the classroom and my reputation. I was indeed viewed as an "interloper" (Moody, 2004). The

students wanted me to respond as if I were White, but I would never be White nor am I culturally white. Second, institutional structures supported my admonition without due process. I was informed of the complaint when the students requested I be: in the next quarter. The institution supported the stereotype of the "angry black bitch," who would seek retribution against the students. I was a sapphire. Deborah Gray White (1985) contends the stereotype of sapphire alludes to the out-of-control, innate lasciviousness and irresponsibility of Black women—it is a historic model. Are students and colleagues more comfortable with the "angry black bitch" stereotype rather than a Black woman who is competent? Or do they prefer an Aunt Jemima character? In that non-threatening role, I would listen and do whatever it took to please my White charges. I would have no power. Third, policy needs to be enforced. Faculty or staff should not allow students to bend the rules when it comes to how they address faculty of color. Students lie. The faculty members should not have to prove their innocence to the institution. Rather students should have to prove they followed policy and procedures and respected the rights of the faculty member. My experiences in the academy speak to the continual life of racism embedded in the cultural and institutional milieu of the academy just as it is in all of our society. It is not a "For Whites Only" kind of racism; it is more subtle and consequently, more dangerous. And acknowledgment of its existence is a start. I suggest we start there.

Since attaining tenure in 2003, each year, I receive less and less recognition for my teaching, research and scholarship. The research contends that African American women can attain tenure and promotion. However, they are often stuck at the associate professor level. As my experiences have shown, I am viewed as a racialized entity within the racist institutional and cultural structure of the academy. In 2007, I presented portions of this chapter at a qualitative research conference; one of the participants in the audience commented that "You are very brave." At the time, I had no idea what she meant. I responded I was not brave; I was just speaking my truth. She insisted that I was brave. How others view this unveiling of the mask will depend on how they identify, understand and either support or deconstruct racism in all of its forms in higher education. In closing, let me share with you how I concluded my journal entry on "Bending the Rules."

> "So, as I look back over my bouts with racism, sexism, and other isms in the academy, I am still wondering when people are going to be explicit about the rules that they do not follow for Black folk in the academy. Just tell me that these are the rules, but there are hidden rules that apply to you…. Do not leave me believing that the rules of academic freedom, social justice, equality, equity, and fairness apply to me… [Make explicit that] we only want this institution for happy sambos, so please do not try to act competent. And finally, we will always maintain our power by any means necessary." At least then, I will not be hurt. At least then, I will not take the evil, vile, vindictive behavior as a sign that something is wrong with me, but as an indication of what the institutional structure is for me as a Black woman. At least then, I can be free to do what only I can do: live.

I want to **live not just survive** in the fullness of who I am as a Black woman in the academy. It may be "unconscionable" to some of my former students, but I have no desire to go elsewhere. I seek my humanity, equity and justice. This can be accomplished, but it means acknowledging that there are rules—written and unwritten—that are embedded in the culture of the academy. My experiences were bound by institutionalized racism, White privilege, and White supremacy interlaced with culture. I believe African American women need the academy to acknowledge their experiences as Black *and* female. Consequently, their evaluations, interactions with students and policy need to be consciously examined from our position(s), not yours. An acknowledgment of our multiplicity will allow us to not only be more engaged in the academy but allow the academy to be more supportive, honest and protective of us.

References

Apple. M. & Buras, K. (2006). *The subaltern speak: Curriculum, power and education struggles.* New York: Routledge.

Caraway, N. (1991). *Segregated sisterhood: Racism and the politics of American feminism.* Knoxville, TN: UT Press.

Clarke, A. E. (2005). *Situational analysis: Grounded theory after the postmodern turn.* Thousand Oaks, CA: Sage.

Collins, P. H. (2000). *Black feminist thought: Knowledge, consciousness, and the politics of empowerment.* New York: Routledge.

Creswell, J. W. (2007). *Qualitative inquiry and research design: Choosing among five approaches* (2nd ed.). Thousand Oaks, CA: Sage.

Delgado, R. (2001). *Critical race theory: An introduction.* New York: NYU Press.

Delpit, L. (1996). The silenced dialogue: Power and pedagogy in educating other people's children. In *Facing racism in education* (6th ed.). Beauboeuf-LaFontant & D. Smith Augustine (Eds.). Cambridge, MA: Harvard University Press., pp. 127–148.

Eastman, P. D. (1998). *Are you my mother?* New York: Random House.

Ellis, C., & Bochner, A. P. (2000). Autoethnography, personal narrative, reflexivity: Researcher as subject. In N. K. Denzin, & Y. S. Lincoln (Eds.) *Handbook of qualitative research* (2nd ed., pp. 733–768). Thousand Oaks, CA: Sage.

Ellison, R. (1995). *The invisible man.* New York: Random House.

Farmer, R. & James, J. (1993). *Spirit, space and survival: African American women in (White) academe.* New York: Routledge.

Foster, M. (1996) *Black teachers on teaching.* New York: New Press.

Freire, P. (2000). *Education for critical consciousness.* New York: Continuum.

Greenlee, S. (1969). *The spook who sat by the door.* Detroit, MI: Wayne State University Press.

hooks, b. (1994). *Teaching to transgress: Education as the practice of freedom.* New York: Routledge.

Hull, G. T., Scott, P. B., & Smith, B. (1982). *All the women are White, All the men are Black, but some of us are brave: Black Women's Studies.* Old Westbury, N.Y.: Feminist Press.

Irvine, J. J. (2003). *Educating teachers for diversity: Seeing with a cultural eye.* New York: Teachers College Press.

Lemert, D. & Bahn, E. (1998). *The voice of Anna Julia Cooper including a voice from the South and other important essays, papers and letters.* Lanham, MD: Rowman & Littlefield.

Locke, M. E. (1993). Is this America? Fannie Lou Hamer and the Mississippi Freedom Democratic Party. In V. L. Campbell, J. A. Rousse, & B. Woods (Eds). *Women in the civil rights movement: Trailblazers & torchbearers, 1941–1965* (pp. 27–37). Bloomington: Indiana University Press.

Lopez, G. & Parker, L. (2003). *Interrogating racism in qualitative research methodology.* New York: Peter Lang.

Lorde, A. (1984). *Sister outsider: Essays and speeches.* Trumansburg, NY: Crossing Press.

Moody, J. (2004). *Faculty diversity: Problems and solutions.* New York: Routledge Falmer.

Parker, L., Deyhle, & D. Villenas, S. (1999). *Race is—race isn't: Critical race theory and qualitative studies in education.* Boulder, CO: Westview Press.

Pollard, D. S., & Welch, O. M. (2006). *From center to margin: The importance of self-definition in research.* Albany: SUNY Press.

Popkewitz, T. S. (1998). *Struggling for the soul: The politics of schooling and the construction of the teacher.* New York: Teachers College Press.

Smith, B. (1980). *Toward a Black feminist criticism.* Brooklyn, NY: Out & Out Books.

Smith, W. A., Altbach, P. G., & Lomotey, K. (2002). *The racial crisis in American higher education: Continuing challenges for the twenty-first century.* Albany: SUNY Press.

Takaki, R. (1993). *A different mirror.* Boston: Little, Brown and Company.

Vargas, L. (Ed.) (2002). *Women faculty of color in the White classroom: Narratives on the pedagogical implications of teacher diversity.* New York: Peter Lang.

Ward Randolph, A. (2000). Race, class and gender in the academy. *HUArchivesNet.* [The electronic journal of the Moorland-Spingarn Center, Howard University], 4. Retrieved August 17, 2009, from HUArchives.Net database.

White, D. G. (1985). *Ar'n't I a woman? Female slaves in the plantation South.* New York: Norton.

CHAPTER SEVEN

"We Are Not the Same Minority":
The Narratives of Two Sisters Navigating Identity and Discourse at Public and Private White Institutions

Ayanna F. Brown and Lisa William-White

Abstract

Autoethnographic[1] research, experimental narrative[2], and Critical Race Feminism[3] were employed here to illustrate the complexities, and at times, conflict between the authors' identity and *minority* status, and the *minority* issues touted as essential to social justice initiatives within and beyond their respective campus departments. Enacted here are the stories of two sisters, both of whom pursued careers as teacher educators at predominantly White institutions (PWIs) within departments that articulate a commitment toward social justice. A methodological discussion of these complexities is interwoven through the narratives, illuminating how the Academy; the paradigm of White women faculty at one PWI; and a patriarchal, "Latinocentric" culture within a department at State WI, all act in concert to promote marginalizing discourses in the context of race and gender. Additionally, the authors illustrate how their familial bond and shared academic interests allow them to navigate these circumstances, and create support systems within, and beyond the dynamics of their departments, universities, and the academy.

Prologue

I AM [Lisa]

the older one.

not the eldest, but the second oldest;

bookended exactly three years between two sisters.

Significant is birth order in the process of *Becoming*.

Second children are unfettered!

Permitted to traverse rough waters un-chartered.

Intellectual curiosity, like maps, are navigational aids.

Books, like sisters, are best friends;

Pen and paper supply the sword to slay demons!

And bouts of self-exile freed me to perfect my prose, to think, to ques-

tion…

My Fears

My Thoughts

My Dreams

My Reality!

I soon discovered,

I WAS

The angry Black girl desiring to live

O-U-T-L-O-U-D

DAMMIT!

My destiny was neither defined by my single-parent home,

nor by poverty!

Food stamps and public housing subsidies taught me

to reject mediocrity,

to reject the shroud of ignorance,

to QUESTION AUTHORITY.

And to debunk all those perceptions stifling equity.

School Counselor, you fail to hear the desires of my soul!

My goals lie beyond the boundaries of what your mind can envision,
Teacher!
I beg your pardon, but your deficit paradigms about Black achievement have
yet to meet
MY APTITUDE Professor!

Don't you know that I never came to the academy kickin' and
screamin',
but screamin' I did do!
And WILL DO!
CAN'T YOU HEAR MY VOICE?[4]
See, never forget,
for Black girls like me,
I
flower in an urban sea,
where possibilities are endless,
For what I can Be.

I AM
The first to go to UNIVERSITY,
To catapult through the academy;
two BAs, an MA,
AND
3 babies,
To earn my Ph.D.
by age 33.

I AM [Ayanna]
the younger sister—the youngest child—the "baby."
I look like her,
I sound like them,

We are alike—all come from resilience and pride.

I am not her.

I am not them, either.

I am bold, unapologetically willing to try, driven while trying
and smile while doing it.

And them, they love me but call me "being just her."

It doesn't feel like a compliment, but in spite of it and sometimes
them, I will be me

NOT them.

Escape the trope of follower—he look alike—the last one

*Yes, we all had the same English teacher, the same science teacher, went to
the same high school. I know you know my sisters, but you don't know me.*

"Ayanna, Black colleges are not as good as White colleges. You won't
get the same resources or support. The expectations are low and you
won't get a job. As your counselor, I would strongly advise you to
consider other offers."

E-S-C-A-P-E

Go to a place where all black bodies are not the same.

Black people can be smart rather than regarded as "exceptions," if
they succeed.

Tuskegee, Howard, Morehouse, Dillard, Spelman, Xavier, I can be me
and not the me you want to put on your catalogue as a trophied black
body that "made it" despite your system that never intended for me
to "make it."

*And why doesn't the counseling center have ANY information on ANY of
these schools? Typical!*

Ahhhh (I exhale slowly with my eyes wide open rather than closed)

Finally, learning to learn, learning to be me, among people NOT de-
voting time to programming me.

After graduation, I went back to that counselor, principal,
"The Academies."

"I got into Harvard, Columbia, Vanderbilt, and U Penn. Just thought
I'd let you know what my BLACK college did for and with me."
In actuality, I applied only to the top four graduate programs as a symbolic
"screw you" to all of those
who seemed to have so much to say about HBCU's but didn't teach me a
damn thing when they were my teachers.

Teach so my students won't get what I got.
Develop the power of words so they can dazzle and suffocate all in
one stroke.
"Powerful people cannot afford to educate the people that they oppress, be-
cause once you are truly educated, you will not ask for power. You will take
it."[5]
The mantra I give my students the words I live by.
I am not angry at all.
I don't have any expectations that you will regard me well because
you never have.

Placing a Round Frame on a Square Window: Our Methodological Considerations

Enacted here are our narratives; two very different sisters who are
very much alike sharing most things, even coded languages that stu-
pefied the rest of our family; we also envisioned careers as educators.
With the limited number of African American women in the academy, the astonishment *for others* that two Ph.D.s come from the same
household may require pause. However, we recognize that our individual and collective trajectories toward becoming socially and politi-
cally conscious and intellectually steeped was not only a blessing but
inevitable.

As sisters and teacher educators with a commitment toward social
justice, language use between us is not simply a means of "catching

up" on life turned *right-side up*; but rather, it is a recursive construction that is as dynamic as our relationship. Because *our worlds* are both academic and familial, there is constant code-switched discourse that creates a comfortable yet untidy continuity between sisterly support and critical scholarly engagement. We are multidimensional as African American intellectuals, mothers, wives/partners, and sisters who rely on multiple discourses to *quiet the storm*. Our discourses are part and parcel of our literal and symbolic sisterhood. See, Ayanna [in the Midwest] and Lisa [on the West Coast] share weekly, demonstrating how our lived experiences are enacted. We often strategize effective ways to support each other, and essential to that support is writing. As such, our emails and Facebook accounts supply a cornucopia of scholarly exchanges and data that frame our experiences and intellectual pursuits. Similarly, our journals consistently provide a format to express our thoughts and feelings related to incidents that emerge within the academy. Thus, we employ autoethnographic research, experimental narrative, and Critical Race Feminism (CRF) in this chapter to illustrate the complexities, and at times, conflict between our identities and *minority* status, and the *minority* issues touted as essential to social justice initiatives within and beyond our respective campus departments.

In constructing this chapter, we grappled with the methodological consideration of language usage and authentic representation. We recognize that the academy rigidly defines epistemology and then prescribes what the appropriate discourse is to illustrate ways of knowing. We also recognize that we live in a culture that essentializes notions of what African American female discourse should look like, and even what speech between sisters must sound like. So here, we disrupt all those normative conceptions. In doing so, our readers will not find a strict adherence to an *informal voice* and *colloquial speech* assumed to be used between siblings. *Rather,* we utilize a round frame for our recursive co-narrative, befitting an intentional attempt to show how we integrate all our Englishes[6] and all our writing modalities and in an authentically non-linear way.

Finally, we chose CRF and some salient aspects of it in concert with Critical Race Theory (CRT) to frame our writing. While teachers and researchers have committed themselves to exploring and expanding constructions of "race" as broader social issues, there are greater challenges for teacher educators to make these issues practical and accessible for praxis. One of these challenges, when trained as both a researcher and practitioner, is to keep your research questions "close to the ground." In the context of CRT, that would mean allowing the voices of the disenfranchised or those who are historically marginalized to speak for themselves. In order to deconstruct how systemic marginalization and privilege impact students, teachers, and communities, teacher educators walk the line of "tearing apart" the very systems that were created on principles of marginalization based on race, language, and gender. So, what does this mean when the academy requires certain criteria for demonstrating professional productivity? It means battling the complexities, "the system," while simultaneously explaining to [it] that [it] is flawed. In so doing, "race work," "race scholarship," and communities that centralize oppression become marginalized when the academy prescribes the context and the content for discussions of race, gender, and the intersections of both.

Email

Yanna [nickname], I love what you wrote and believe it should be kept for the reason that we are "Framing Our Story" and how our narratives show how we are situated, which contextualizes our EXPERIENCE in the academy. Poetic form condenses what we would otherwise say, inauthentically, in too many words. Look at the abstract again! We are framing autoethnography. Key here! So the data collection process, written form and function used to craft the narratives are important, and how we got [to the academy] are critical, I think. We can reevaluate later. XOXOX

Lisa

Strange Fruit on the Equity Tree: Narrating Our Experiences

Lisa's Adjunct Hiring Experience

The professor with whom I have been working this summer says, "You MUST come work in my department!"

"What… is your department?" I ask.

She explains, "It existed as an area group for three decades but fought to become a department. It caused a battle in the college. The result: 51 to 49 to establish a department." White folks pulled out the heavy artillery. Even the copy guy's vote counted. Bad blood.

She goes on to add, "The department is race/language conscious, big on educating Chicanos, migrants and Spanish bilingual teachers. Department members testify before the State legislature to advocate for English Language Learners. Over 75% percent are students of color, with the majority being Latino. White students, like all of our White faculty, are usually bilingual (Spanish)." I think to myself, proud history! Framed! Given to every cub who comes there and unknowingly enters the lion's den. This was clearly a demonstrative, political effort to promote politics in the department title—BILINGUAL.

Some of the old lions marched with the United Farm Workers. I saw a photo on a desk of a professor sitting at the knee of César Chávez.[7] Paulo Freire[8] even stopped by for a visit! As I laugh I jokingly think, shit, anybody 'round there hang out with Gandhi or Mandela? Yes, I'm intrigued!

I am scheduled to come in during the summer for a casual meeting with the department chair to talk about their part-time teaching needs. When I arrive, I immediately notice the murals adorning the walls: César Chávez , Frida Kahlo, Che Guevara, Dr. King, Malcolm X, Mother Teresa. My interest in this department was further heightened. This is actually a place that appears to align, at least viscerally, with the liberation pedagogy that I espouse. A good beginning here, I think.

However, when I enter the chair's office, there are FOUR professors—two Latinos, one man and one woman (an Asian male and an African American male). Then the barrage of questions begins, "What do you know about Multicultural Education and/or Social Justice? Who are scholars you admire? What is your research focus? What teaching experience do you have Do you speak any other language…What is…? How are...?"

I was caught off guard. I was NOT informed that this would be an impromptu committee interview! YES, I AM on the defensive. I had to put on my mask.[6]

Then I begin my spill, "Multicultural Education is…I have an affinity for …My dissertation research was…Yes, I have taught in diverse settings…Yes, I am bilingual; I speak Black English Vernacular if you consider the socio-political context of language usage…." I can see that my quip pleases by their wide-eyed nods and smiles.

Then the Latino male says, "Let's cut through all the b.s. here now! I have been sitting here looking at this resume for weeks. A sistah[7] who actually has a teaching credential and can teach English Language Arts methods, who has an M.A. in TESOL (Teaching English to Speakers of Other Languages), TESOL! Do you know how rare that is?" Aaah, the trope of the exception. Yes, the exotic "other"![8]

He continues, "I just wanna know this: What is your worldview?"

I am taken off-guard and perplexed, "Worldview?"

"Yeah, worldview?" he says. Everybody is silent for what seems to be an eternity, and I am confused. What is he expecting to hear? That I was trained at Highlander; rode with the Freedom Riders in Mississippi; was there at the March on Washington in '63!?!?!?

"WHAT ARE YOU ABOUT?" He asserts.

Aaah, got it! He is unable to reconcile. Young and Black, single mother, A.B.D. from a top-tiered PWI.[9] Irritated by ambiguity AND tone, I begin, "I grew up in…bussed, tracked…crack began to destroy my community… graduated pregnant…learned to endure in the face of adversity" blah, blah, blah….

He interrupts, "NOW THAT'S WHAT I'M TALKIN' 'BOUT… WANTED TO KNOW WHAT KINDA SISTAH YOU ARE, especially comin' from that white-ass university."

Laughter fills the room. The Latino male flippantly waves his hand to suggest that he is done and finally proclaims, "I'm good ya'll. No more questions." They all smile and nod to show approval.

Hell, was he trying to see how down[10] I am? Wondering if I might be some assimilationist Negro subversive? How can people be so cavalier about propriety and protocol when hosting an impromptu interview with racial overtones? Shouldn't multiculturalists know a little somethin' somethin' about Affirmative Action/Equal Employment Opportunity regulations? UNBELIEVABLE! Then I ponder, who, or what, is the sacred cow here? Me, as a Black woman? They, as a predominately minority, majority-Latino department? Or the boom this department offers to the university's diversity statistics?

Several old sages say, "There were two Black female prospects many years ago." Identity and ideological conflict shut their doors, I heard often around the water cooler.

Hmmm, if hired, what will this look like? Moreover, what will be the expectation?[11]

The Culture of Lisa's Department

Over the past eight years, I have often been reminded that I am a visitor in *their house*. This means that in a department where, at our peak, there were 21 faculty: 2 African Americans; 9 Latinos (all of whom speak Spanish); 4 Asians (two of whom have some Spanish language competency); and 6 Whites (all of whom are Spanish-bilingual and several of whom are either married to Latinos, or have spent extensive time immersed within Latino communities), there is a dominant department culture and world view that reflects the knowledge, values, and experiences of Latino cultures. Coupled with the faculty demographics and our focus on the needs of linguistically diverse populations in California's K-12 schools, my department has earned an "unofficial" reputation in the College of Education as a "Latino" department. This view is so pervasive that many non-Latinos, and monolingual students are often surprised to learn that they can *also* pursue a teaching credential in our program.

As a Black female within a largely minority department, and embodying a strong activist orientation for the needs of all marginalized communities, particularly African Americans, I, along with a few others, have worked to expand my department's focus on the needs of *other* communities. This often includes a disquieting dialogue. To capture the range of these issues, I created a montage from journal entries—an epic poem that frames several critical incidents from department meetings since 2000:

I watched…waited…carefully, absorbed the culture, the rules. Copious notes I'd take; like Geertz[12]. Our department retreats used to have a vacation-like vibe. Toasts to hard work, strategize for the upcoming year. No wine these days to free inhibitions. The verbal joust years back went too damn far.

"Fuck that White boy" and "We can settle this outside punk" were yelled with reckless abandon. But why is he being picked on? Whether said in jest or not, we are all wondering how the topic of "White women having flat asses" and your "ethnic preferences" for whom your son marries fit into that lecture? The majority of Latino-student-witnesses may have found the rants humorous; may have marveled at a professor's academic freedom, but was it humorous when outed by those White female students? When they spoke to their White male program coordinator; then to the White female department chair; then to the White female associate dean; then to the White male University Equal Opportunity/Affirmative Action Officer, how did that feel? I know we stress to students on Day 1 to keep grievances "in house" and "follow the chain of command." That they did, but were dissatisfied with the outcome.

And when those White women wanted to be transferred to another instructor's class, some faculty (mostly Latino) vehemently protested; said that their issue was endemic of White resistance to dialogue about racism. *Racism? STOP already! Let's look at the systems of domination here. Why are we ignoring the master narrative of "male privilege" that makes sexism invisible in this conversation?* "Forgotten here are students and their rights to learn in an environment safe from 'isms' in various forms. Forgotten here is how a tenured faculty member is in a position of power, and is part of a protected class." My years working in Student Affairs provided me with another lens to view this issue.

My comments were unwelcome; my positionality questioned. TOO STEEPED IN NATIONALISM; PATRIARCHY! Wrap up ideologies with a social justice ribbon. Justify all discourse as challenging WHITE PRIVILEGE.

I am told by a Latino, "Remember, a White man is still a White man when he is in YOUR house!" This means White faculty can be allies in efforts focused on social justice, but their White identity and privilege still makes them outsiders in the department. This has been said several times, and stated vociferously after another one of those tumultuous department meetings.

Here, some faculty choose muteness as camouflage! Unfree or too weak to challenge. *How can White faculty argue with minority faculty when the White racism and privilege card gets thrown on the table? Dilemma!* Other folks also silenced by nepotism and rhetoric wrapped in BRAVADO. But silence or blind allegiance also makes you culpable MUJERES![13]

Those pathologies in our department were not atypical. Ever since these arguments or silences, there have been factions. Robert's Rules of Order for Parliamentary Procedures go right out the window during these times. Two junior faculty women couldn't take the machismo; one quit, the other went on an extended leave. For a year! A new hire cried after a meeting, ridiculed for sharing ideas no less. She? Another "other." It isn't her house, so she shouldn't be challenging their ideas.

So I sharpen my ethnographic eyes, throw caution to the wind, and don't apologize for MY tongue when I speak up. I am tired of this shit! "There's a DIFFERENCE between passionate dialogue that encourages solution seeking, and debate that silences."[14] I said this through a late-night email when the silence became too debilitating. I am bothered by the tornado that upsweeps all in these meetings. There is a huge elephant on the table and everyone tap dances around it. I wanted the dialogue to continue; I wanted to hear the ideas of some of the silent "others"; I wanted the dialogue to be constructive and not come to a halt because someone has thrown down the pro-verbial White privilege card. Then I received a trickling of late-night email responses from colleagues. The most notable was, "Wow! Admire your bravery. I always shut down in those situations. Reminds me too much of my father."

COWARD! You call yourself a feminist? I think as I read her words. Her email to me is a subversive act: She aligned with that faction who controls the keys to the kingdom. Must be sad to have to compromise one's integrity to fit in, I think as I read her words. They didn't want her in the department either. SOLIDARITY, RIGHT? WRONG!

Student Voice and Curricular Content in Lisa's Department

Students' views about curricular content fuel the arguments at meetings too. At one of those meetings, a White colleague said, "When White students enroll, I tell them that they are guests here. This was in response to some White students' concerns about how they are represented. "This program is a place for minorities to feel affirmed," my colleague continued. Is that supposed to explain to White students why the dominant discourse here about Whites speaks only of racism and privilege? Shouldn't multicultural education affirm all engaged in struggles against domination? Plurality of perspective?

"We need to expand the ways that we analyze oppression in all of its forms here," I share.

After *Lau vs. Nichols*[15] the Chinese students grew in numbers, raised their voices; made a place for themselves. And the department responded by offering Bilingual Education (Cantonese). Asian faculty were hired and the students' needs were central in the department. They are gone now; their numbers have not been substantially reflected in the program's demographics for years.

Now, the Black M.A. students question the relevancy of bilingualism and second language acquisition in their program emphasis. They are not credentialed teachers; many of them work in group homes, juvenile court schools, alternative settings as paraprofessionals. Places where too many disenfranchised Black kids are. Since these educators now know what culturally relevant is, they want it applied to their non-traditional educator's curriculum. They call for Afrocentric pedagogy. But, accommodation is contentious! This pedagogy lies outside of people's knowledge-base and comfort zone.[16]

"We are already inclusive of African Americans in our advocacy of multicultural/social reconstruction," some faculty say aloud; some mutter comments under their breath, EN ESPAÑOL! During a meeting a motion is made, "Let's eliminate that pathway from our program altogether."

"To do so would virtually eliminate Blacks from our department!" I tell them. But few seem impressed. Meta-message: BLACK students, like White students, must be GUESTS here TOO.

WHAT? ALL OF YOU PEOPLE gained rights off the blood and sweat of MY PEOPLE! But I can't share that view—it reeks of my own prejudice; it's too divisive; puts US against US. Where is our commitment to race-conscious/language-conscious policy decisions?

In the college, African American grad students organize. Ask me to support their efforts to push for our own program—For US by US.

"Not doable ya'll," I tell them. "But, I'll push for greater inclusion here!"

"No stand-alone course focused on one group's interest here," a White colleague says. My colleague conveniently ignores the tradition of tailoring courses to students' needs, and hiring faculty that reflects both our mission and student demographics.

You all have to be fuckin' joking! I think. We have Intro to Bilingual Education courses almost exclusively taught by Spanish-speakers; there's a Hmong Literacy course. Cynically I think, I guess ya'll threw that bone to the Hmong so that we can keep Multicultural in our department name? I reject a one-size-fits-all model for teaching and learning.[17]

I CALL FOR A CRITICAL RACE THEORY EXAMINATION OF THE NON-LATINO EXPERIENCE IN THIS PROGRAM!!!

Developing Courses: Ayanna's Experience

I read Lisa's narrative about the culture of the department, and it is so clear that when any group engages in meaningful struggle to decentralize power, unless they are making a deliberate effort to also analyze their own power, they then can create new forms of oppression. The silos of power that create new cultures are endemic when the powerless are all struggling for some form of liberatory hope. Hmmm. I think my own experiences, while less explicit than Lisa's, are far more nuanced in both tone and intention. For me, the vulnerability I presently experience is tempered by the fact that I am not tenured. And so, while I offer these expressions, I am cautious because the context for these events is critical for a more elevated discussion of race, gender, and cultural discontinuities that mediate them both when they are intersected. Let me explain…

Opportunities to develop new courses and to create new learning experiences abound. The campus thrives on ingenuity that is shared among faculty and is supported within the department. Students are encouraged to consider new courses. Yet, there is a troubling sense of complacency within our students' attitudes about learning. It's rather odd because they will do whatever you ask of them as long as it is a requirement for graduation. So, the creation of new learning experiences is held captive to the common discourse of "does it count?" In return, we all develop courses with hopes. And those courses that discomfort complacency, expose issues of power and privilege, and challenge students toward self-reflection and empowerment don't stand a chance. Here I explain:

Journal Entry Thirty-Three
Course syllabus. Learning contract. Dynamic learning contract. It moves as the needs of the group move. Education. History. History of education. Oppressive. Devaluing. No change. Course complete. Walk away. Give grades. No change. Create a course. A new course. Require some greater intellectual stimulation and sociohistorical grounding in whiteness, otherness, race, racelessness. Do the identity work of why. How? To whom? GREAT! "What a wonderful idea, Ayanna. Submit a proposal for a class. An elective." An elective? *But no class currently takes these issues on in our program; elective?* I do. Course submitted. Accepted. Wait for students to sign up. Only need 8 students in the whole department. This is going to be great. Transformation. Address systemic oppression and equity. Registration. One student enrolled. Keep waiting. Two students enrolled. Keeping waiting. Three students enrolled. Registration is almost over. Surely these issues are important to transforming inequity. *Is no one here interested in transforming inequitable systems?* Keep waiting. No one else signs up. Now, not only is the course not required, it doesn't get offered. Only three. Social justice. Education. Transformation. Social Reproduction. White students will become White teachers. No change. I have got to get this course to become required. How? To whom do I approach? "Our students' course loads are already so full." I can hear it now. Justification for the lack of social, racial, economic, and culturally transformative courses in education.

Students Complain. Leadership Listens. Ayanna Repositioned.

When I moved from home at eighteen, left California for Alabama solely relying on the strength of my family. They were intangible, but always accessible. One of my "off to college" stories is how our older sister required that I call her every time the Greyhound bus stopped along the 2½ day ride. I called collect, staying on the payphone all hours of the night ensuring Lorraine [18] that no strangers were following me and that I was alright. Yet, despite the sanctity of that relationship, I was alone. As a recourse, I used journaling as a way to write my fears and concerns; to make sense of non-sense. And yet, sixteen years later, I still write when I feel alone.

Journal Entry Sixty-Six

Sixty-six days later, here I am, writing in this damn notebook saying what I should have said aloud. And you really want to know why 'Black people tend to shout?' No you don't. Wiley[19] had it right when he penned that title. I am mad. Pissed off. Mad. My head hurts, and for all feelings of confusion that consume me, I am more angry with myself. How could I not speak up? How could I not speak out and check her? She was goading me into the very constructions of blackness and black womanness that I oppose, and I saw it happening as I avoided the net. Yet, I still clinched my teeth together, creating a fake-ass grin holding in my words. But inside, I wanted to scream.

"Ayanna, what could you have done differently?" She slants her head slightly to the left while pretending to jot down meaningful notes on her yellow pad.

I then cautiously responded, "Nothing." "I wouldn't have changed anything, if I may be quite honest. My instructional choices were pedagogically sound. And when privileged people complain, we need to evaluate both the complaint and the context in which these concerns are raised. As a matter of fact, I communicated to you weeks ago about the class tone, her tone and her temperament. So, now that she has "complained," you are asking me what I would have changed?" I didn't shriek or skip over my words. Do you realize that Black women in the academy experience student complaints at alarmingly greater rates than both Whites and Black men? Are you seriously asking me what I would have changed? Maybe I would have giggled a little more often or played the mammie role for them so they would see me as "nice." You want me to indict myself by suggesting I've done something wrong. What did I do, teach? I showed up as a prepared, engaged, challenging, and well-versed teacher educator/researcher as I was trained to be. What would I have changed? P (uh) lease.

But this is not the source of my soreness, my pain, my ache, and the rebellious tears that ran down my cheek. *Shit! I don't want to be sitting here sniffling and wincing as if I am weak! I am not.* Lisa and Lorraine will tell you, I've always had the strength to cry when I am mad. I grew up a "cry baby." That's how strong I was then, too. Little do you know that you are better off to see me cry than to hear me speak, because IF (pause) I (pause) CHOOSE (pause) TO (pause) LET (pause) THIS (pause) OUT (long pause) (heavy breathing with brand new tears rolling down staining the page of this notebook)...

"We can talk again next week when we have more time." *I don't have anything else to say. I don't agree and rather than asking me what I would do differently, ask them how they are using the evaluation process as a means to cajole me into giving them a better grade cause, according to you,* "Graduate students don't get Cs." *Aren't Cs average? You mean every graduate student stompin' round here is exceptional? That is amazing. How did we pull off this crop of crème de la crème?* And these complaints are the result of the fear of getting less than a B. I HAVEN'T EVEN GRADED THE FINAL PROJECT YET!

But I have to sound agreeable, so I stupidly reply, "Let's consult our calendars and plan a chat. Let me know when you are free." And then, here it is the other 'she' with her do-gooder manipulation...In retrospect, this was "good cop/bad cop."

"You know, Ayanna, you are smart. You are articulate. You know how to do good research. Maybe you let them know how smart you are and that you've done all this work so you can put them in their place. You know...maybe you are intimidating."

Did she really say that? Was I supposed to co-sign this subversive attempt to get me to say, "Yes. I do want to put them in their places." I am watching your eyes squint like I am being slowly hypnotized and will spew out at the top of my lungs, in a BLACK rage....I WANT TO PUT THEM IN THEIR PLACE AND WIN. THEY PISS ME OFF! I stared at her in disbelief.

"No, I don't think that, nor do I need to say that."

I AM ANGRY AT YOU. Not them, you. For all of your "social justice," "women's rights," "fight for what you are worth and get paid" blah, blah, blah. You just tried to play me!

Intelligent, Articulate, Thoughtful Research equals Intimidating. To whom? Them or you? So, because of these characteristics, **I** am Intimidating? And so, that justifies this complaint that has taken up one hour of my life that I could have been using in other ways? The products of my hard work, isolation, and inquiry are reduced to this...Is this your opinion? Do **you** feel intimidated by me...Are you threatened by my intelligence, oratorical delivery, and research agenda? Are you suggesting I begin to re-evaluate my...character? My head still hurts. Tears still being defiant. Damn. I know she saw me trying to wipe my eyes. I let her get the best of me and said nothing. Let me just walk out before I choke.

"Let's talk again next week. Oh yeah, Ayanna, the graduate students mentioned that you brought your daughter to class on two occasions." At that moment, I reflect on a conversation that we had during my campus tour. She began, "Ayanna, this campus community has really come along way. When I arrived, the administrators were all men. Oh, you would have no idea what work we had to do, what fights we had to patiently fight to get where we are today. For example, the child care center was not really seen as a priority, until one of them needed child care. I remember in the department, we younger faculty with young children would bring our children with us to work and we would just watch them [the kids] for one another. We made it work for each other."

This reflection makes me smirk at how hypocritical this is. I respond, "No. I brought her to my class on one occasion, and on the other occasion, I was sharing my research with another class. I contacted the professor in advance, and she assured me that bringing the little one wasn't a problem. Is that a problem?" *What the does my daughter have to do with any of this? Is this your nail in the coffin comment? Adding insult to injury.*

"Well, yeah (pause). We can't bring our children to class. It's a liability issue. I know we hadn't really talked about this before, but if you can't make childcare arrangements..."

"I don't have a childcare arrangement problem," *I would have never brought her to campus for an evening class or presentation if I had not gotten the clear indication from you that I could.* "This isn't a problem. No worries."

Now my head is pounding. If I write any more, I will likely not go to work tomorrow. Then maybe I will fulfill the 'always late' or 'no show, no work' ethic stereotype of Black people that you seem to need to feel better about your liberating Whiteness. Always fighting.

Pen down. Lights off.

Epilogue: Analysis & Final Considerations

After reading and re-reading each other's journals, poems, and talking between classes via cell phone, we decide to use the ease of email conversations to determine the most appropriate method to elucidate our enduring ideas, and even marvel at the unexamined, insidious nature of racism and sexism when actualized by *so-called conscious* people. We sift through our numerous email exchanges, and continue our recursive process of shooting emails back and forth as we generate new insights.

> Email
> …[Yanna] your minority status is complex; yet, the word complex belies adequacy…You raise some important tensions that demonstrate your racialized and gendered positionality. I find this scenario disconcerting, and eerily familiar, White privilege, embodied in White students' complaints, engender a discourse that results in your marginalization in several ways. Your grading process is questioned; your motivation suspect. When we spoke before, it was clear that a White alliance positioned you in opposition—"Black" professor who wants to "put [White people] in their place." Are you supposed to embody a vendetta? Collegiality and professionalism masqueraded as code, and a warning notice for you! Then you were left to stew in veiled insults. On another note, I am compelled to call you Sojourner cause "aint you a woman" too? Isn't it ironic that the same battle cry used by those feminists to fight for recognition of their family needs is an issue raised to admonish you? Though an invalid issue in your case, that part of your narrative shows how power had to be exerted in some way to put your uppity Black self in your place. In all, you illustrate what bell hooks calls "interlocking systems of domination."[20]

Then Ayanna responds:

Email

Lisa, I really enjoyed your inserts. I felt like I could see ya' face. You know—the Lisa stuff you do when you pissed off but can't say, so. Won't say so. The fluttering of your eyes like the wings of a hummingbird. ☺

What is most compelling is how you remind us that just because you all are "of color" in that room participating in the culture of power,[21] there are still ways of engaging that should not be violated just because we are supposed to be "down." You know, when I originally text-messaged you my idea for this chapter, "We are not the same minority," I wanted to capture that oppression is complex and not merely the acts of faces, but that of ideologies.

…You really capture the tension in the department retreat culture that was created by limiting the various voices. What power dynamics or "fear" might have been created through the silence or silencing of White people in the department because they were White? …You have [also] spoken about how you balance, as an African American woman, an overwhelming focus on Latino Liberation in a Multicultural education program that attempts to use resilience and history to create new paradigms for what critical theory teaching and learning looks like. All the while, the de-emphasis on race empowerment for all racialized communities has created a new racial hierarchy within your department (e.g., a limited if not ignored amount of academic work being done for and about disenfranchised communities, more broadly).

What is particularly striking is you challenge the paradigm of what social justice looks like? You push the boundaries and expose the multiculturalists of their own prescript for revolutionary/anti-oppression pedagogy… Interesting… I hope folks reading this can dance this sociopolitical tango that you've created.

We then decide that beyond the issues examined that we did need to resolve our desired approach about analysis:

Email

[Yanna]…and as for analysis, and maybe this is rhetorical, but is it really necessary for us to explicitly analyze for the reader all the nuances of how discourse within our departments serves to marginalize? I ask because narrative research allows the writer to interpret a reality for the reader through the discussion and analysis of the emergent themes within text. But Evelyn (2004) argues that poetic narrative is a form of analysis as it does not overwhelm text with scholarship, and it is a legitimate form that generates data/knowledge. Mackie's (2009) piece is a POWERFUL example of autoethnography, using systematic sociological introspection rather than analysis for some intended audience.

Also, might there be a passivity embedded in the relationship between the writer and the reader when ways of knowing and understanding lie only in what the writer tells the reader he/she should take from a narrative—almost like the writer is omniscient and the reader cannot generate thought? I state this because I think the writer of poetic/experimental narrative should also advocate for the reader to bring some independent analysis to a text; positioning how the reader can interpret and form conclusions. Thus, there are themes, nuances and subtleties related to race and gender that our reader will also bring to these narratives. An epistemological shift for researchers to consider, perhaps? Implied in Evelyn (2004) is an argument that this type of relationship can exist between writer and audience and also between family members (Lachman, 2009). ☺

Lisa

We both agree that our readers will bring valuable insights to their reading of our narratives, which leaves us both satisfied. Then, a last idea is sent in an eleventh-hour email:

Email

Lisa. While your explication of autoethnography and the role of reader, text, and audience is clearly dynamic, what you don't discuss is how the opportunity for interpretation [of issues of race and gender] when utilized for publication presents challenges for those of us who are *untenured*. I agree, the poetic form gives the writer the creative opportunity to divulge issues, particularly in this case, with Black females in the academy, that might remain silenced; or [those who write about these experiences] withhold these talks, only to be discussed among their colleagues, *sistahs in the academy*, who will "get it," and will not hold it against you as intellectuals who "couldn't play the game." I think this work requires further intellectual rigor in the academy to pay attention to its own framing of scholarship, social interactions, professional learning communities, use of language, departmental policies; and moreover, include an active examination of the representation of what and who constitutes a minority.

I sure am lucky to have a sister/sistah in the academy.

Love you & thanks for playing with me, yet again.

Ayanna

Notes

1 See Bochner (1994), Ellis (2004), and Ellis and Bochner (1992, 2000).

2 Evelyn (2004) suggests that experimental narrative forms, such as poetry express collective experience in concise and unique ways not exactly replicated by direct quotes, case studies or even other narrative forms" (p. 106). See also Richardson (1999), pp. 660- 668.

3 Critical Race Feminism is a framework where both race and gender, in concert, deepen the analysis of Black female academics' positionality; see Crenshaw (2003).

4 Coming to voice is an act of resistance as bell hooks cites on page 12 in *Talking back.*

5 John Henrik Clarke (1985)

6 Amy Tan in her essay "Mother Tongue" writes of her experience, as a Chinese American author toward integrating all of her Englishes within her writings to capture "her intent, her passion, her imagery, the rhythms of her speech and the nature of her thoughts."

7 César Chávez founded the National Farm Workers Association which later became the United Farm Workers.

8 Paulo Freire, renowned Brazilian educator and influential theorist of Critical Pedagogy.

6 Rodriguez (2006) argues that "masking ourselves can serve the need to conceal part of our identities, essentially serving our need to survive in a racist and patriarchal world," (p. 1068).

7 Black woman

8 Gary Howard suggests that social dominance theory frames how a dominant group legitimizes myths and exacerbates the social positions between the "majority" group and subordinate groups—a powerful marker of creating a "we" and a "they" positionality. See Howard's *We Can't Teach What We Don't Know.* New York: Teachers College Press.

9 bell hooks (1990) argues how Black people must challenge essentialist, one-dimensional colonial notions of Black identity. See "Postmodern Blackness" in *Yearning: Race, gender, and cultural politics,* Boston: South End press, p. 28.

10 A colloquialism for expressing one's commitment to a cause or issue.

11 Madsen and Mabokela (2000) cite Kanter who discusses how underrepresented individuals may be perceived as tokens in organizations, may be subject to performance pressures to ensure maintenance of the normative cues of the organization, and may be subjected to polarization and exaggeration of these differences.

12 Clifford Geertz is a famous cultural anthropologist whose work focused on interpreting the symbols he believed give meaning and order to people's lives.

13 Silence is not influenced by one's tenure status, as associate and full professors are those referenced here.

14 Taken from "A Framework on Dialogue vs. Debate" by Shelley Berman, Dialogue Group of the Boston Chapter of Educators for Social Responsibility. More information may be obtained at http://www.esrnational.org/

15 *Lau. v. Nichols* decision required schools to take "affirmative steps" to overcome language barriers denying children's access to the curriculum. Congress immediately endorsed this principle in the Equal Educational Opportunity Act of 1974.

16 See Howard's *We Can't Teach What We Don't Know* for further discussion about the tension of preparing to teach diverse populations.

17 Gloria Ladson-Billings (2009). Fighting for our lives: Preparing teachers to teach African American students, In Antonia Darder, M.P. Baltodano, and R.D. Torres (Eds.), *The critical pedagogy reader.* (pp. 460–468). New York: Routledge. She suggests that the educational needs of African Americans are generally couched in deficit paradigms; that scholarship delegitimizes African American culture; and that generic models of pedagogy that teach Black students in a culturally neutral manner are ill suited.

18 Lorraine is the oldest sister; oftentimes, the other mother.

19 Wiley, Ralph (1992). *Why black people tend to shout: Cold facts and wry views from a Black man's world.*

20 bell hooks (1989). *Talking back.* Boston: South End Press.

21 Lisa Delpit.

References

Berman, S. (2009). Framework on dialogue vs. debate. Paper prepared for the Dialogue Group of the Boston Chapter of Educators for Social Responsibility. Retrieved June 19, 2009 from http://www.esrnational.org

Bochner, A.P. (1994). Perspective on inquiry II: Theories and stories. In M. Knapp & G.R. Miller (Eds.), *Handbook of interpersonal communication* (2nd ed., pp. 21–41). Thousand Oaks, CA: Sage.

Clarke, J.H. (1994, November). Education for a new reality in an African world. Paper presented for the Phelps-Stokes Fund. Retrieved May 23, 2009 from http://africawithin.com/clarke/education_for_a_new_reality.htm

Crenshaw, K. (2003). Demarginalizing the intersection of race and sex. In A. Wing (Ed.). *Critical race feminism: A reader.* New York: New York University Press.

Ellis, C. (2004). *The ethnographic I: A methodological novel about teaching and learning autoethnography.* Walnut Creek, CA: AltaMira Press.

Ellis, C., & Bochner, A. (1992). Telling and performing personal stories: The constraints of choice in abortion. In C. Ellis, & M. Flaherty (Eds.), *Investigating subjectivity* (pp. 79–101). Newbury Park, CA: Sage.

Ellis C. & Bochner, A.P. (2000). Autoethnography, personal narrative, reflexivity: Researcher as subject. In N.K. Denzin and Y.S. Lincoln (Eds.), *Handbook of Qualitative Research* (pp. 733–768). Thousand Oaks, CA: Sage.

Evelyn, D. (2004). Telling stories of research. *Studies in the Education of Adults, 36*(1), 86-110.

Freire, P. (1970). *Pedagogy of the oppressed.* New York: Continuum.

hooks, b. (1989). *Talking back.* Boston: South End Press.

hooks, b. (1990). *Yearning: Race, gender, and cultural politics.* Boston: South End Press.

Howard, G. (1999). *We can't teach what we don't know: White teachers, multiracial schools.* New York: Teachers College Press.

Lachman, M. K. E. (2009). Dreams of my daughter: An ectopic pregnancy. *Qualitative Health Research, 19*(2), 272–278.

Ladson-Billings, G. (2009). Fighting for our lives: Preparing teachers to teach African American students, In Antonia Darder, M.P. Baltodano, & R.D. Torres (Eds.), *The critical pedagogy reader.* (pp. 460–468). New York: Routledge.

Mackie, C.T. (2009). Finding my...a story of female identity. *Qualitative Inquiry, 15*(2), 324–328.

Madsen, J.A. and Mabokela, R.O. (2000). Organizational culture and its impact on African American teachers. *American Educational Research Journal, 37*(4), 849–876.

Richardson, L. (1999). Feathers in our cap, *Journal of Contemporary Ethnography, 28*(6), 660–668.

Rodriguez, D. (2006). Un/masking Identity: Healing our wounded souls, *Qualitative Inquiry, 12*(6), 1067–1090.

Wiley, R. (1991). *Why Black people tend to shout: Cold facts and wry views from a Black man's world.* Penguin Books: New York.

CHAPTER EIGHT

Women and Minorities Encouraged to Apply:
Challenges and Opportunities of Critical Cultural Feminist Leadership in Academe

Alicia Fedelina Chávez

Abstract

This chapter explores the leadership experiences of a Mestiza in higher education. Teaching stories are used in the tradition of Spanish and Native American cultures to illustrate some of the ways of being, challenges, and opportunities of a woman of color negotiating predominantly White and predominantly Spanish and Native American collegiate institutions and communities in the Southwest and Midwest.

> We must live life as full, authentic, human beings, living honorably and sharing responsibility for seven generations into the future.
> Wilma Mankiller, former chief of the Cherokee Nation

What does it mean to be a woman of color and also a leader in academe…to be *Mestiza* (Spanish and Native American) and to be someone who influences others as a critical cultural feminist? A colleague and friend once observed after an instance when I was acting as a catalyst for change in a university, "You are an activist disguised as an administrator." I am still puzzled that these two roles of activist and administrator would be interpreted as separate since in *Mestiza* culture, leadership and administration are forms of activism meant to influence things for better for our own and all people (Anzaldúa, 1987; Chávez, 2009). I am a woman whose two cultures have been blended since the mid-1500s when my Spanish ancestors emigrated to what are now the small towns of Taos and Luiz Lopez, New Mexico, intermarrying with Indigenous tribal members (Beck, 1962) and blending Native and Spanish values, norms, beliefs, and traditions into a new culture that is *Mestizo y Mestiza.* Those who visit Taos, my home town in the northern mountains of New Mexico, often remark that they feel as though they have traveled to another country because the rhythms of life are so very different from what they are used to in their individualized and frantically busy lives elsewhere. We have a favorite saying in my family that I now know originates in Spain, "We work to live, not live to work." My sisters often remind me that my work is not who I am; that I am more than my work could ever be so not to get too caught up in something as insignificant as an individualistic career. I am encouraged to make my work about serving others, especially those who need that service most. A favorite Taos T-shirt reads "Carpé Mañana!" — "Seize Tomorrow!" and we laugh about how life is too precious for manifest destiny or competing to get ahead. Success in my home town is often defined as being whole, spiritual, connected daily to those you love, part of something larger than yourself, and immersion in the small beautiful activities of everyday life. Though I come from a very large family of professionally successful individuals, each of us has made choices to give up greater professional success to stay or return to be with our extended family and live within the deep rhythms of New Mexico. I keep these rhythms with me as a critical cultural feminist leader, teacher, and scholar in academe.

Students, colleagues and friends often tell me that I am "an old soul" and I wonder what they mean. Some try to explain that I work from a deeper and wider perspective in congruence with the quote at the beginning of the chapter about responsibility for future generations or that I seem to know inherently where we need to go to become a blending of diverse epistemologies and practices in higher education, or that I see cultural possibilities and patterns across academe. I have been asked by faculty how I know cultural, critical, and feminist theory so well, and after much study, I am now able to explain to them that these are not theories that I learned in a book, they are ways of being from my culture, from the gender-cultured *Mestiza* practices of women as warriors, leaders, philosophers, healers, teachers, and scholars. My "old" cultural ways of being are considered "new" ways in academe. Indigenous (Grande, 2004; Green, 2007; Villegas, Rak Neugebauer, & Venegas, 2008) and Latina feminisms (Brown & Strega, 2005; Cordova, 1998; Garcia, 1995; Elenes, González, Bernal & Villenas, 2001; Trujillo, 1997) are now espoused as new ways to critique and transform society, and yet these epistemologies have been in the world for a long time and include ways in which I was raised. Black feminist thought (hooks, 1989; Lorde, 1984) and many Asian feminisms (Baker, 1997) are also considered newer to academe yet are very old and serve as foundations for cultures that were around long before their popularity in academic paradigm and scholarship. I find this strange paradox of old and new both comforting and confusing as a leader and scholar. Since I didn't learn these epistemologies from books or theories or research articles, I think about them in very everyday, pragmatic terms and for a long time was unaware that there were epistemologies and theories "proposing" some of my ways of being to academe and to United States society. For most of my life I have lived these epistemologies without being able to quote from theorists or even be aware they might be considered

"alternative." In living within Indigenous and Latina feminist paradigms, I often seem incredibly different to most I work with in fundamental ways as a leader, teacher, and scholar. And though the
phrase "women and minorities encouraged to apply" is so common-
place as to be almost invisible in descriptions and ads for positions in
academe, I find that most of the time, professionals and students
around me want my ways of being in theory but not in practice. In
practice, my old ways of being are often considered irritating, incon-
venient, and unwanted regardless of my effectiveness as a leader,
teacher, and scholar or my cheerful, friendly, and optimistic demeanor.

What I know is that as a leader, teacher, and scholar, I often see
the gifts in others that they do not yet see in themselves, and I move
forward in my work with them to cultivate and encourage their use
for the transformation of higher education to a more diverse epistemology and practice. I can see so clearly in my heart's eye, the possibilities of each individual contributing to the collective. I often
contemplate what we could be if each of us were to move beyond
rhetoric and truly turn our gifts toward becoming a diverse academy,
a diverse world in spirit and practice. I find that when I lead as
though this were already true, magical things can happen...we can
and do become the best of who we are. Yet there are also the ugly, the
insidious structures of power, and those who benefit greatly from
them and are comfortable within the status quo of academe. I have
experienced this ugliness as a woman of color from my first leadership role as a very young residence hall director all the way to serving
as a dean of students for a big 10 university and then leading a small
rural highly diverse college campus in my home town. My goal has
always been to diversify our epistemology and practice so that we are
able to draw from the wisdoms of many identities and epistemologies.

From a critical cultural feminist perspective, leadership in higher education is such an intrinsic thing. It has to do with our ability to be catalysts for our own and others' "becoming." It is leading and learning as ways of being (Chávez, 2009). My leadership effect is often greatest when those I lead don't realize that they have been influenced, when they believe in their own abilities to do great things in part because I have challenged them to know themselves, to think outside of themselves, push the edges of the way things are, and trust in their own gifts to see them through. Women of color often go unsung as leaders (Velarde, 2003) because like our mothers before us, we are brash yet subtle, infinitely strong warriors, nurturing, pushing, urging, encouraging the best in others in ways that build self-knowing, self-actualization. We quietly rejoice as each of those we lead goes out on their own to influence others, to make a difference in small and large ways. Whether we are teacher leaders, administrative leaders, mother leaders, healer leaders, or scholar leaders we are warriors—strident, determined, passionate and creative to whatever extent is necessary.

My dedication to and passion for the transformation of higher education toward a more diverse epistemology and practice were forged from early educational experiences of my own and in my family, honed from witnessing struggles of collegiate students and professionals from less common identities in the academy, and burnished by theory, research, and practice. It is no great surprise to anyone in my large extended family that I chose to return home as a collegiate leader and then teacher/scholar after many years in other universities. For as I wrote earlier; I am a daughter of New Mexico and live within her rhythms. In this essay, I utilize autoethnographic teaching stories gleaned from 25 years of anthropological observations and reflective journals to illustrate some of the vast challenges inherent in serving as a leader and woman of color in academe.

Critical Cultural Feminist Leadership, Teaching, and Scholarship

This autoethnographic study and essay was developed from a critical cultural feminist epistemology, a term I use to describe a collection of principles serving as a foundation for my leadership, teaching, and research which are drawn from tenets of critical theory, Latina and indigenous feminisms, and critical race feminism. I embrace ethics and philosophies as a professional in higher education including: 1) integrating mind/spirit/body/heart, 2) applying a constant inward and outward anthropological eye to strive toward deconstructing and recrafting gender-cultured norms of higher education, 3) living a sacred responsibility of care, compassion, and empathy, 4) activist scholarship, leadership, teaching, and writing, 5) power with rather than over others, 6) creative expression and passion within a rigorous practice, and 7) hopefulness in the possibility of individual, institutional, and societal transformation. I choose to study and write about identity borderlands in leadership so that we may understand our similarities and differences more deeply in the service of transformation and effectiveness in academe. From feminist theory, I embrace a personal and relational approach to practice (Mohanty, 2003); from critical race feminism I embrace the notion that data from heart, mind, body, and spirit are essential to practice (Wing, 2003). From critical theory, I apply critical deconstructive approaches in the tradition of Derrida (Kearney, 1985). Anthropological deconstruction and critique are helpful to understanding values, assumptions, and beliefs underlying leadership and institutional practice especially where identity privilege is a key factor (Fried, 1995; Ibarra, 2001). Consistent with Latina (Garcia, 1995) and Indigenous (Green, 2007; Grande, 2004) feminist philosophies I believe in taking a hopeful stance that it is possible for society to become more socially just (Elenes, González, Bernal, & Villenas, 2001). I critique for both what is problematic and what is helpful about the gender-cultured norms of higher education and leadership. In keeping with indigenous feminist practices, I choose to write in an integrated, woven means to study cultural borderlands within leadership and institutions for the purpose of collegiate transformation (Anzaldúa, 1987; Green, 2007; Wing, 2003). From both indigenous and critical race feminism (Green, 2007; Brown & Strega, 2005) and from autoethnographic research (Ellis, 2004) traditions, I blend data from heart, spirit, mind, and body in scholarship by processing emotions, applying an ethic of self-study to role model this important process for all leaders. Last, I use teaching stories to offer a comprehensive and holistic sharing of findings and draw from Indigenous and Spanish traditions of influencing through story.

Autoethnographic Teaching Stories as Catalysts for Transformation

I began keeping autoethnographic notes and reflections originally to assist me as a woman of color to make sense of culturally foreign collegiate environments and as a form of stress relief. It wasn't long before I became interested from a perspective of educational anthropology and social action. I noticed that my field notes and reflections had the distinctive anthropological eye of much of my scholarship about higher education, and I deepened my techniques and observations even further. Daily reflections of culture and extensive use of teaching stories common in my extended family provide me with tools that have continued to serve me well as I negotiate educational environs based in the cultural norms of others. I continue, however, to be regularly astonished at how invisible many of these norms are until I suddenly bump painfully into one in my work. These continuing instances urge me forward as a scholar and writer to continue delving deeply into the intersections and divergences of cultured and gendered norms and to assist others in understanding them through teaching stories. By relating experiences from my own leadership as a cultured, gendered outsider, I hope to engage readers cognitively and emotionally and contribute to continued positive social change and transformation of academe. The following are a few teaching stories of how I have successfully and unsuccessfully negotiated between cultures as a leader in different roles at three different universities, the University of Wisconsin-Madison (UW), where I served as the dean of students, University of New Mexico-Taos (UNM-Taos) where I led the campus as the executive campus director, and Iowa State University (ISU), where I served as diversity development specialist, providing training for faculty and staff and consulting with colleges and university departments on diversity. UW-Madison is a Big 10 predominantly White institution in the upper Midwest, UNM-Taos is located in my home town and is a very small, predominantly His-panic and Native American rural branch campus of the state's flag-ship university, and Iowa State University is a large land grant predominantly White institution in the Midwest.

Students in Need: Balancing Old and New Ways

This story may seem typical to many who work with students, and yet I have found that few professionals in higher education consider how processing aspects of identity can vitally assist students in nego-tiating small and large dilemmas of student life. In addition, our cul-turally individualistic orientation in this society can have a chilling effect on support networks available to assist students. Over the years, I have struggled to remain myself as *Mestiza* while honoring and yet pushing the boundaries of gender-cultured policy and prac-tice. I have long been uncomfortable working in a realm of regulation between individual privacy and familial inclusion. In both of the cul-tures I come from, an ethic of involvement is expected. I sometimes describe this in myself as my intrusive nature as a teacher, leader, and friend. My learned tendency is to inquire about private things, call or visit those I'm worried about, and connect with family and friends of those in trouble. Laws governing student rights to privacy make some of this impossible, and yet I believe that students benefit from the supportiveness of those they trust. Many students we work with suffer all by themselves, keeping their hurts, disappointments, fears, and needs tightly hidden inside. Over the years, I have developed practices that create a balance between privacy and supportiveness, individuality and collectivity. I have also developed ways to ask about identity to assist students more fully. I describe one situation while I served as dean of students in the following excerpt.

> Yesterday I met with a White male student who seemed very distressed in the quiet way I've come to recognize as common among males from this state. I closed the door and asked him how I could be of assistance. He gave me a relieved look and told me that he had just lost a close friend to suicide, was failing his courses, and was having his own thoughts about committing suicide. After listening for awhile I asked him a question that I have developed over time, "Are there aspects of your identity, such as being male or circumstances such as where you grew up that are impacting this situation for you?" He looked at me with astonishment and then told me of how he was the first in his extended farm family not only to attend college but to finish high school. Tears rolled down his cheeks as he shared that his family had pooled their money to send him to college and how could he be a man and face telling them he was failing. I asked him who among his family, community, and/or friends he felt safe with, who did he trust. Once again, he looked relieved and talked of an uncle he was close to.

I spent the rest of the time with this student assisting him practice calling his uncle first to talk through his situation and gain support in then speaking to his parents. I asked him if he would like to call his uncle from my office so I could be with him for moral support. He did so and we went over some campus resources he might use. I ended by walking him personally to the student counseling center for a preliminary session. After many years of working to balance the cultural norms of my upbringing with the parameters of academe, I believe that we need to work within the constraints of systems even as we push them to evolve. By assisting students to identify support people in their own lives and consider identity and background aspects of situations, we can facilitate more effective solutions and offer deeper assistance. Especially while working in the Midwest, I have in a number of cases been confronted by other professionals who believe that asking questions of identity is getting too personal and that I should let students tell me what they are comfortable sharing. Yet identity is so much a part of how we relate to the world and I believe that we must continually push the highly gender-cultured boundaries between the personal and public to serve students.

Envidia: Negotiating Latino Politics as a Woman

When I was hired to return home after 20 years away to lead UNM-Taos, a small branch campus of the state's flagship university, I knew that I had challenges ahead. The first two campus leaders were male, and there were few women in any type of leadership positions in town or county education or government. My father warned me about the Latino politics of the community, and my mother cautioned me about *"envidia,"* a common practice of pulling others down from high places in many oppressed communities (Anzaldúa, 1987). I had heard that coming home is never easy and had seen my father struggle with his return after 21 years of military service. There is a strong history in my ancestral home of distrusting outsiders and those who leave behind the humble professions of their home communities. Centuries of broken treaties and commitments have made it common to trust a handshake more than a signature and someone in the community more than someone from outside (Beck, 1962). I quickly found that people around me displayed one of two reactions, either thrilled that I was there as a daughter of old families of Taos who was now experienced and had the title of doctor or deeply distrustful of my legitimacy as a leader who is a woman of color. A critical difference from my past collegiate experiences was that I was now in a community and college in which more than 50 percent of the residents and students are of Mestizo, Hispano, or Native American heritage. Another difference is that gender role separations are even stronger than anywhere else I have served. All-male tribal councils are common in the governments of the Indian Nations of this state, and the two local public entities I worked with most, the Town Council and the college advisory board were each made up primarily of Hispanic males. I remember feeling excited to come home culturally and yet concerned at being such a public female leader within local gender-cultured role expectations. Though it is difficult to critique already oppressed cultures in this nation, unequal treatment of women is common to and yet manifests differently across cultures (Garcia, 1995; Green, 2007; hooks, 1989). It is important that we, as women of color, make visible some of the ways that gender is used as an oppressive identifier in our cultures. An early excerpt from my journal of this time reads.

> I know from my own upbringing in this community and the critical foundations of relational connections normative in Latino and Native communities that it will be essential for me to make clear my connections to others with stories of my extended family and my education in the Taos Public Schools. This will ease the development of trusting partnerships with community leaders for college initiatives and student success.

A second entry a month later,

> Today I spoke at my first Town Council meeting after requesting time on the agenda to introduce myself. I started with a story of my own education and the wise local familial and school teachers who were essential to my own growth as a professional and human being. To signal the importance of many kinds of livelihood and knowledge in this rural community I spoke of

being able to birth a sheep, make enchiladas, conduct and publish research, and lead important initiatives. I must honor both what has been and the possibilities of the future. As is my habit, I wore a long bright skirt and adorned myself in silver and turquoise, long ago moving away from the common business suits of academic leaders. I could see that these symbols of community and identity were connecting as people throughout the council and audience nodded and murmured support. Several council members made a point to connect themselves to my family. I noticed, however, that unlike responses to male leaders introducing themselves at the same meeting, some of the responses to me seemed to be a "pat on the head." Comments implied female roles that I might play on the campus such as developing childcare, enhancing teaching, and nurturing students. Even after I spoke of my work as a dean in a large university, one council member offered to be of assistance in areas he assumed I had no experience such as finance, construction of the campus, and legal issues. He continued in subsequent meetings to offer to assist me in these areas even when I discussed my experiences in each and learned that he had little experience in any!

Throughout my remaining years as the leader of UNM-Taos, I experienced many situations such as this and was able to invoke some of the matriarchal leadership of Hispano and Native cultures to lead which include arenas such as family, community, and spirituality. I became known over time as "patrona," a female version of a male leadership role as I stood my ground, stepped forward, and invited others to partner with me for the benefit of our community.

Grandmothers, Mothers, Sisters and Great Aunts: Finding Wisdom along the Way

As I looked into those wise and beautiful eyes across the table over lunch, I listened in awe as this tiny, full of life woman from very old cultures of China offered graciously to serve as an aunt during my time of campus leadership at UNM-Taos: "It is very presumptuous of me, yet I would like to offer to serve as an aunt to you as you lead this campus. Long ago, I was a leader and a warrior in my own country and internationally and now I am a healer and artist. I know that it is painful and challenging to lead as a woman in a male world...even more so when we are from cultures other than the majority in this country."

During my four years leading this small, rural, multicultural campus, I called on this humble, gentle aunt for support, for advice and to return from a sense of crazy making that often comes with leading in the borderlands as a woman of color. I let go of some old patterns of thinking, found peace amidst the chaos, and discovered new resilience in myself because of this gentle warrior from a country and culture far from my own. For me it is natural to reach out to elders, not only those who are older than me but also to those who carry specific wisdom that will assist me in serving others.

During my first days in office as dean of students for the University of Wisconsin-Madison, I was faced with the duty and daunting privilege of calling the parents of a student who had died the day before. Being childless myself, I wondered what I could say to offer comfort to parents facing an incomprehensible loss. Though I had dealt many times with student deaths on campuses, I had never had to represent a university as the first and primary contact in this kind of situation. As a person of collective mindset, I did something almost immediately. I called my mother who is a natural healer for those facing loss and spoke with her for over an hour. What I heard was that mostly I needed to *still* myself to listen, encourage these parents to *care for themselves* as they cared for others, and to *offer support in small ways*. I remember seeing my hand tremble as I punched in the numbers to call these parents. As I introduced myself, I felt blessed and terrified simultaneously to be a part of these moments in the life of a family. Like most of us, I imagined how I might feel if this were my loss and felt again some losses of my own. When I introduced myself and both parents got on the phone, I began to hear a story other than the one I'd been told, and the situation curved into an even more complex and devastating one than I had prepared for. I learned that, unlike what I'd been told, this couple's son had not died in a car accident but rather had committed suicide and died in his father's arms. I gave silent thanks to my mother for encouraging me to still myself and listen, for if I had said any more in my introduction, I would have created an even more difficult situation. As I found over time, and is often the case, these parents wanted to share their son with me. For the next 45 minutes I listened to stories about this bright young spirit, to the painful perplexity these parents felt from their son's final act, and offered what solace I could in being present with them. I cried with these parents, offered assistance when they were ready with negotiating anything related to the university, and encouraged these two individuals to care for and be kind to themselves even as they guided others through the many rituals of laying someone to rest. I encouraged them to call me if they would like to talk again and thanked them for their generosity in sharing some of the life of their son.

Though I had been calm through the discussion, as I often am in a crisis, I began to tremble after the phone call. And once again, without hesitation, I reached out for the wisdom of an elder. The day before, I had met an incredible Navajo woman from my home area, who is a healer in the student counseling center at the university. I felt an immediate connection to her when we met, and I picked up the phone and took a chance that she might be in her office. Amazingly, I was able to get through and she agreed to meet me. I told her of my phone call and asked her if she might be willing to be a personal connection for me to reach out to when I was preparing to facilitate a difficult situation and for debriefing afterwards. I told her of the situation I had just dealt with, and she offered comfort, wisdom, and support in a time that was difficult for me. She reminded me that it is the way of collective peoples to reach out immediately to others during challenging and joyful times and I felt less alone as a leader.

I would encourage others of any identity not to hesitate to reach out to elders and others who can be present with us, offer advice and company along the journey as leaders and as women of color. What we do as leaders is challenging and can be painful. There is no need to be the heroic, stand-alone leader. I believe that we do our best work when we reach out for the wisdom and company of others.

Leading Across Cultural Rhythms

Cultural rhythms differentiated from one part of this nation to another serve as a real challenge to leaders who are from less common backgrounds. I find that one of the most important things I do to be effective as a leader is to learn these norms and learn to negotiate them in ways authentic to me as a *Mestiza*. In the Midwest for example, I found that male professionals always started with the "business" at hand and were not likely to bring up anything personal during a meeting with me (Barak, 2005; Gardenschwartz & Rowe, 1992; Thomas, 1992). Though I have developed ways to bring in the personal at some point in a meeting, I learned over time that many males from Caucasian American ethnic groups connect through common interests and goals in their work, and that by honoring and engaging this kind of connection as well as bringing in the personal, I can advocate and partner with them in service to students. With Hispanos, my upbringing holds me in good stead as I know to start by asking after families, referring back to something we talked about in a previous meeting to reinforce connections, and letting the business of our meeting begin when the conversation naturally moves in that direction. With Native professionals, I find it important to make time for formal introductions, blessings, and periods of silence. It is appropriate and expected in many Native communities for individuals to form connections by sharing clan, tribal, and familial relationships.

Though I am not from a specific tribe, I make sure to introduce myself with the four maternal and paternal names in my family, mention our family's long history of ties to the land through sheepherding and to protecting our way of life as warriors in the military.

The Dilemma of *Not* Successfully Negotiating Ethnic Patriarchy

Lest my focus on successes in negotiating situations as a leader give readers the impression that this chapter is a romanticized perspective on working across differences, I'd like to share some situations in which I did not succeed. In every leadership position I dealt painfully with issues of difference in which I was unable to negotiate ethnic patriarchy successfully. Early in my professional life, I applied for and was offered a position as a diversity development specialist in the training and development department of Iowa State University. My role was as diversity consultant and trainer to faculty and staff in colleges, departments, and the larger university. Though there are many things I'm proud of having accomplished while in this position, the following story from 1993 serves to illustrate the institutionalized challenges of influencing individual leaders and organizational transformation amidst ethnic patriarchy.

> Today, I met with the president of the university in my capacity as a member of the Presidential Task Force on Diversity. My goal was to share concerns and offer alternative perspectives about his public statements announcing that he would not support partner benefits for employees. I decided after consultation with members of the Lesbian, Gay, Bisexual, Transgender (LGBT) Faculty and Staff Association and Diversity Task Force members to try to place this issue in relation to historical policies affecting the rights and benefits of other underserved populations. I shared with him historical situations of African American students not being able to graduate because of university policies that kept them out of certain academic activities required for graduation such as swim classes that did not allow them to enter the pool and so prevented them from final testing. I related these to a

burden of some university employees having additional stress from worrying about health and other benefits for their partners and the impact this was likely to have on their ease of functioning within the university. The president lost his temper at this point and yelled at me for being too young to understand and as a 'spic' [derogatory term for a person of Latino origin] how could I have a sense of the political realities of leadership. He stated that he had only created my position as a public salve to those pushing for diversity and that I should just focus on offering workshops and let real leaders go about the business of making decisions about the university.

In this situation, I underestimated institutional resistance of individual leaders to deeper transformation, the politics of change efforts, how much individual values and belief systems make up a leader's choices, the tokenism of some hiring and diversity initiatives, and how to use my scope of influence most effectively. In looking back, there are many things I might have done differently such as requesting that the president meet with the whole task force rather than trying to go it alone, considering this individual's worldview, and contacting possible cultural translators to the president prior to proceeding. Yet the outcome is likely to have been the same given this particular leader. In this situation, I may have shown moral courage (Kidder, 2005) yet lacked the necessary professional savvy and understanding of another leader's agenda and personality to have the most influence. In addition, I have learned much more about how deeply cultural and gender norms are institutionalized and now know more about looking for small and large indications of readiness for change in both individuals and groups. Lastly, I didn't take enough into account how much my own identity and position might be a factor in how I was perceived by the president. We must each consider how we are perceived by others and work at ways to remain authentic and still deal pragmatically with the realities of others' perceptions. With whatever scope of influence we have, we must often "nudge and wait, nudge and wait" (J. Chagnon, Personal Communication, January 2006). In addition, we must be willing to face the frustrating reality that many people benefit from the way things are and will resist in subtle and overt ways. Our dilemma is to keep learning ourselves so that we can act effectively as transformative educators and leaders.

Another way in which I have continued to struggle in working as a leader across differences is to come painfully up against supervisors and chairs who became actively uncomfortable with my practice as a woman from a *mestiza* way of being. I find that ethnic patriarchy is not present just among men and I have to struggle with it in myself as well as in others. In three situations, my supervisors or department chairs were Caucasian American women born and raised in the Midwest, and their professional expectations came up against both my own and my expectations of them as elders. Each of these dilemmas came as a surprise to me because these leaders were women and I expected a more relational orientation. Each situation took place during formal evaluations. The following serves as one example.

> I finally feel able to write about a painful and confusing situation I dealt with last week. I had my formal evaluation and after raving about my work and telling me that my work with students, supervisees, and projects was outstanding and 150%, my supervisor carefully set aside my evaluation paperwork and began to tell me that I would be even more productive if I would change my professional practices to be more like hers. She went on to explain that the time I was taking to chat with folks first thing in the morning as well as the time I took to get to know personal aspects of colleagues and supervisees would be better spent on projects. I froze in silence, not knowing what to say. Even later when I tried to explain that this relational and personal sharing time is critical to my 150% productivity, I stumbled over my words and felt lost in confusion and betrayal. How could someone who talked so much about diversity not support it in practice? How did she expect me to work more effectively if she insisted I leave behind one of my most effective tools?

Like many people, for me the most difficult and heart-wrenching negotiations across differences are those with whom I feel I should have mentoring/elder relationships. In the traditions of women in both my cultures, I have been taught that those in positions of authority serve as a form of elder and hold a sacred responsibility to me as a mentee. Though I find it easy as a leader to negotiate with other colleagues and leaders much older and more experienced than I, it is a different matter when they serve as my supervisor, advisor, chair, or teacher. I am also often perplexed when this comes from another woman because I am expecting all women to define relationships at work in the lifelong way that I was raised to assume. I have over the years struggled with a cultural tendency to stay longer than I should, believing in life-long relationships (Chávez, 1998) and feeling confused in negotiating across differences with those to whom I report. My own early lessons of the unquestioned wisdom of elders can both assist and derail my efforts as a leader. Though I began job searching at this stage of most of these positions, my recent strategy in this reporting arena is to consciously reflect and purposefully make choices that balance what is best for me and for those I serve. I am more likely now to fight back with first informal and if necessary, formal action. I have also come to understand that wisdom is defined differently across cultures and is not necessarily a goal of higher education (Villegas, Rak Neugebauer & Venegas, 2008). In the tradition of *Mestiza* feminism, sometimes it is best for me to let my "*Mestiza* warrior activist," self take the center, standing up for myself while knowing that I am also standing up for those who come after me. This is something I still struggle with as both a woman and a person of color. I find it so much easier to stand up for others than for myself. Perhaps this will always be a struggle for me. Even now, in a faculty role, I am facing similar dilemmas and still trying to learn how to negotiate them in a way that is strong, positive, compassionate, and effective.

The End Is the Beginning...

Other strategies I find helpful as I continue to negotiate academe include greeting negative colleagues with positive energy, empathy, and compassion; using my strengths to minimize and compensate for areas in which I'm limited; building up my warrior self by funneling the energy of anger and frustration toward positive purpose; dressing as myself yet formal enough for the occasion; cultivating a positive inner voice (and telling the negative inner voices to be quiet!); replacing competition with collaboration toward shared goals; balancing myself with rest and renewal; and engaging others in the future by enlisting their talents toward common purpose. We each embody multiple identity cultures that need to be part of a diverse epistemology of higher education and with each new year I gain new insights and strategies to also consider identities such as class, sexuality, religion, age, and ability. It is clear to me that we must engage our whole selves as leaders, teachers, and scholars if we are to negotiate these gender-culture borderlands and successfully serve a diverse society. I believe the common pressure to ignore, devalue or deny heart, body, and spirit in much of academe challenges our evolution as collegiate organizations operating in a global context. Imagine the possibilities as we embrace who we are as warriors, mothers, leaders, activists, teachers, healers, and scholars.

References

Anzaldúa, G. (1987). *Borderlands, la frontera: The new Mestiza* (2nd ed.). San Francisco: Aunt Lute Books.

Baker, M. J. (1997). The different voice: Japanese norms of consensus and "cultural" feminism, *UCLA Pacific Basin Law Journal,* 133–147.

Barak, M. E. M. (2005). *Managing diversity: Toward a globally inclusive workplace.* Thousand Oaks, CA: Sage.

Beck, W. A. (1962). *New Mexico: A history of four centuries.* Norman, OK: University of Oklahoma Press.

Brown, L., & Strega, S. (2005). *Research as resistance: Critical, indigenous & anti-oppressive approaches.* Montreal: Canadian Scholars Press.

Chávez, A. F. (1998). Weaving my way: The cultural construction of writing in higher education. [Special Issue on Pressing Issues of Inequality and American Indian Communities.] *Journal of Poverty: Innovations on Social, Political and Economic Inequalities, 2*(4), 89–93.

Chávez, A. F. (2009). Leading in the borderlands: Negotiating ethnic patriarchy for the benefit of students. *Journal about Women in Higher Education, 1,* 39–65

Cordova, T. (1998). Power and knowledge: Colonialism in the academy. In C. Trujillo (Ed.), *Living Chicana theory* (pp. 46–77). Berkeley, CA: Third Woman Press.

Elenes, C. A., González, F. E., Bernal, D.D., & Villenas, S. (2001). Chicana/Mexicana feminist pedagogies: Consejos, respeto, y educación in everyday life. *Qualitative Studies in Education, 14*(5), 595–602.

Ellis, C. (2004). *The ethnographic I: A methodological novel about autoethnography.* Walnut Creek, CA: Alta Mira Press.

Fried, J. (1995). *Shifting paradigms in student affairs: Culture, context, teaching and learning.* Lanham, MD: American College Personnel Association.

García, A. M. (1995). The development of Chicana feminist discourse. In A. Kesselman, L. D. McNair, & N. Schniedewind (Eds.), *Women images and realities: A multicultural anthology* (pp. 406–416). Mountain View, CA: Mayfield.

Gardenschwartz, L., & Rowe, A. (1992). *Managing diversity: A complete desk reference.* New York: Harper and Row.

Grande, S. (2004). *Red pedagogy: Native American social and political thought.* Lanham, MD: Rowman and Littlefield.

Green, J. (2007). *Making room for Indigenous feminism.* London: Zed Books.

hooks, b. (1989). *Talking back: Thinking feminist: Thinking Black.* Boston: South End Press.

Ibarra, R. (2001). *Beyond affirmative action: Reframing the context of higher education.* Madison, WI: University of Wisconsin.

Kearney, R. (1985). Deconstruction in America: An interview with Jaques Derrida. *Critical Exchange 17*, 1–33.

Kidder, R. M. (2005). *Moral courage.* New York: HarperCollins Publishers.

Lorde, A. (1984). *Sister outsider: Essays and speeches.* Berkeley, CA: Crossing Press.

Mohanty, C. T. (2003). *Feminism without borders: Decolonizing theory, practicing solidarity.* Charlotte, NC: Duke University Press.

Thomas, R. (1992). *Beyond race and gender: Unleashing the power of your total workforce.* New York: AMACOM, American Management Association.

Trujillo, C. (1997). (Ed.), *Living Chicana theory* (pp. 352–370). Berkeley, CA: Third Woman Press.

Velarde, L. A. (2003). *Leaders of color in higher education: Unrecognized triumphs in harsh institutions.* Walnut Creek, CA: AltaMira Press.

Villegas M., Rak Neugebauer, S., & Venegas, K. R. (2008). *Indigenous knowledge and education: Sites of struggle, strength and survivance.*

Cambridge, MA: Harvard Press.

Wing, A. K. (2003). *Critical race feminism: A reader* (2nd ed.). New York: New York University Press.

Studies in the Postmodern Theory of Education

General Editors
Joe L. Kincheloe & Shirley R. Steinberg

Counterpoints publishes the most compelling and imaginative books being written in education today. Grounded on the theoretical advances in criticalism, feminism, and postmodernism in the last two decades of the twentieth century, Counterpoints engages the meaning of these innovations in various forms of educational expression. Committed to the proposition that theoretical literature should be accessible to a variety of audiences, the series insists that its authors avoid esoteric and jargonistic languages that transform educational scholarship into an elite discourse for the initiated. Scholarly work matters only to the degree it affects consciousness and practice at multiple sites. Counterpoints' editorial policy is based on these principles and the ability of scholars to break new ground, to open new conversations, to go where educators have never gone before.

For additional information about this series or for the submission of manuscripts, please contact:

Joe L. Kincheloe & Shirley R. Steinberg
c/o Peter Lang Publishing, Inc.
29 Broadway, 18th floor
New York, New York 10006

To order other books in this series, please contact our Customer Service Department:

(800) 770-LANG (within the U.S.)
(212) 647-7706 (outside the U.S.)
(212) 647-7707 FAX

Or browse online by series:
www.peterlang.com